HOW TO

RETIRE

DEBT-FREE

& WEALTHY

HOW TO

A FINANCE COACH REVEALS

RETIRE

THE SECRETS, TIPS, AND

DEBT-FREE

TECHNIQUES OF HOW CLIENTS

& WEALTHY

BECOME MILLIONAIRES

CHRISTINE IBBOTSON

Licensed Financial & Investment Advisor,
Estate Planner, and Tax Specialist

NIMBUS
PUBLISHING LTD.
NIMBUS.CA

Nimbus Publishing Limited
3660 Strawberry Hill Street, Halifax, NS, B3K 5A9
(902) 455-4286 nimbus.ca

Printed and bound in Canada

NB1511

Edited by Barry Norris
Design by Jenn Embree

Library and Archives Canada Cataloguing in Publication

Title: How to retire debt-free & wealthy : a finance coach reveals the secrets, tips, and techniques of how clients become millionaires / Christine Ibbotson, licensed financial & investment advisor, estate planner, and tax specialist.
Other titles: How to retire debt-free and wealthy
Names: Ibbotson, Christine, author.
Description: Reprint. Previously published in 2018.
Identifiers: Canadiana 20190234776 | ISBN 9781771088022 (softcover)
Subjects: LCSH: Retirement income—Planning. | LCSH: Retirement—Planning. | LCSH: Finance, Personal. | LCSH: Retirement income—Planning—Case studies. | LCSH: Retirement—Planning—Case studies. | LCSH: Finance, Personal—Case studies.
Classification: LCC HG179 .I23 2020 | DDC 332.024/014—dc23

Nimbus Publishing acknowledges the financial support for its publishing activities from the Government of Canada, the Canada Council for the Arts, and from the Province of Nova Scotia. We are pleased to work in partnership with the Province of Nova Scotia to develop and promote our creative industries for the benefit of all Nova Scotians.

Dedicated to AZ
Loved forever and always

Never stop dreaming.
Always love more, and...
Remember you can always go further
in every facet of your life.

AUTHOR'S NOTE

This book contains personal accounts and actual experiences of how the author's clients increased their wealth. Names and certain irrelevant facts have been changed to maintain complete confidentiality. This book is intended as a tool that, in the examples provided, proved to be very successful. Neither the author nor anyone involved in the publishing of this book accepts any liability for losses or damages incurred as a result of following the advice and details provided herein as, among other things, timing, personal circumstances, and luck can often play a role in the outcome. Any references in this book to retail banking products, credit rules, banks, investment products, and the like are made only as examples, and in no way are meant to endorse or specifically recommend such tools.

CONTENTS

LESSONS FROM YOUR FINANCE COACH

IMAGINE YOU ARE ON A BEAUTIFUL BEACH IN YOUR MOST FAVOURITE place to vacation. It is a magnificent day—clear skies, warm breezes, and miles of white sand with long views of the crystal blue ocean. At this moment, you have not a care in the world. Your thoughts are clear of financial worry, and the only decision you need to make is whether the waiter should bring you another Strawberry Daiquiri. Is this not how you want retirement to be? Not a care about money, no debt, and the freedom to travel or do whatever you want? Of course, we all want this!

Now back to reality. In today's busy life, most people are worried about their jobs, their kids, and what to make for dinner. Planning for the future is usually last on the list. Most believe it is too difficult to understand all the ins and outs of the financial markets, how to save and plan for the future, and how to pay off their mortgage. They would rather leave it up to someone else to make the decisions on their retirement portfolios. Of course, they haggle tooth-and-nail for the lowest possible rate on a mortgage renewal, and question their financial advisor when their annual fees seem too high and their return is taking a swan dive into the pond of retirement uncertainty. But apart from this, most of us just think it will "hopefully" happen, as though some magical fairy will guide us to retirement and tell us what to invest in to ensure we can retire comfortably.

"I hope I can retire at sixty…maybe not?" Unfortunately, most people wait too long to plan, and then panic.

Today, the majority of people live paycheque to paycheque, and don't seek professional advice to attain their own customized financial plan. They usually think they will be forced into buying an investment product they don't want, or they just don't see the value in having it done. They say they are too busy, and become close-minded to the concept of devising a plan for their future. The fact is that most clients between the ages of thirty-five and forty-nine would have their lifestyles severely compromised, immediately, if they missed only one paycheque for any reason. So, what will happen when you are on a fixed retirement income that is most likely half of what you are taking home now?

Very few clients entering retirement will want to compromise their current lifestyles, but will find it difficult to live on less income, especially if they still have a mortgage or outstanding debt. Even after downsizing and compromising lifestyle dreams, they still find they need to return to work on a part-time basis. Clients without debt also might need to return to the workforce to delay withdrawals from their investment portfolio in the hope it will continue to grow.

Plain and simple, you must create your own customized financial plan. And here in this book you will have all the tools and techniques to save and eliminate debt. Have you ever wondered why other people are debt-free and you're not? Why do they have money and they are not stressed about the future? What did they do? How did they do it?

It is very simple. If you do what other financially successful people have done, you will get the same results. There is no magic bean to plant or pill to swallow. You do not have to have some unique idea to become wealthy. All you need to do is find out how people like you are creating wealth, and copy them! Yes, I said copy them! Find out how others are saving and making money, and do the same thing. You will get the same results! It's no miracle, it's just common sense. It doesn't matter where your finances are now. All that matters are what changes you are willing to make to take control of your future. If you want to achieve a higher level of wealth than you have today, you have to change your way of thinking about money. The fact that others like you have done it and developed the skills for financial success only provides the testimonials you need to develop the same skills too.

Making money, saving money, and having your assets grow is what you are going to learn how to do, from people who have done it and are on their way to becoming multimillionaires. Here, you can read real-life stories from clients who made the right choices and some who even made the wrong choices, so that you can get inspired and take full control of your own financial life and create a path toward wealth and success. You will learn how to get the most out of your investments, how to build and protect assets, and even how to use the banks for your own benefit, not theirs.

The people who are on the right financial plan are those who are constantly moving out of their comfort zone and not leaving their financial future up to someone else. Instead of waiting for things to happen and then reacting, they are improving their situation and creating opportunities for wealth. If you take only one thing from this book, take this: If you are not happy about your financial situation, there is only one person who can change it—YOU!

So, let's get started.

GETTING STARTED

When it comes to planning, most people are unsure and sometimes overwhelmed with how to tackle their finances and eliminate debt. The media and large financial institutions have done an excellent job convincing us that our mortgage should be paid over the standard twenty-five-year amortization, and have ensured we stay in debt by allowing us to acquire more credit in the form of credit cards, lines of credit, and personal loans.

Home renovations, buyouts on car loans and leases, credit card debt, and family vacations are just some of the things most people will consolidate into their mortgage. Banks are more than happy to help ease your worries about debt by providing you with a larger mortgage and extending the amortization out to make the monthly payment feel manageable. We have developed the habit of sweeping the debt "not under the rug" but into our mortgage.

Before we get into our stories of how to build wealth, we should discuss some basics on how we initially advise all our clients to review their finances and their current lifestyle. It is necessary to establish your own CORE Plan so you can take charge of your future, rather than following the advice of bankers and advisors who simply put your future on auto pilot. Using the Trackers will help you not only to isolate unnecessary expenditures, but also to find the funds you need to save and eliminate debt. Once you have a basic understanding of how to plan financially for your current lifestyle, it will be easier for you to relate to the solutions offered in our client stories.

Remember, to reach your dreams you must do the incremental steps over time to get there. Money is not just for toys and possessions; it provides the means for you to reach your goals and ensures your comfort, dignity, security, and independence as you age. Be honest with yourself and be committed to change. Let go of any past indiscretions or setbacks, and start anew with a clear mind toward financial freedom. There is no reason you can't retire debt-free and wealthy. I have seen it happen to hundreds of clients who changed their negative net worth into a million-dollar portfolio. You can do it, and you owe it to yourself to try.

CORE,
THEN
EXPLORE

MOST OF US WERE VERY GOOD SAVERS WHEN WE WERE YOUNG. We saved diligently every month, and even worked extra hours or took on a part-time job to purchase something we really wanted. When we first got married, we saved to buy a home. We did without, we struggled, and we were able to save money every month even though we probably made a fraction of what we earn today. I know, you would never want to go back there. Look how much better you are now. You make more money, you have more assets, and life is better, right? Of course it is.

If that young former self could see you now! If back when you were just starting out you could have looked into the future and seen all that you would accomplish, you would have been really proud of yourself and probably couldn't have waited to get there. But now we have all this stuff, we have lost the skills to save, and gained the skills to buy. We are consumption junkies. We like our toys, cars, and must-haves. We justify to ourselves that it is getting ahead to buy the next larger home, the next car to upgrade, and that "must-have" item for the house or yard. Now, more than at any other time in history, people are using credit far too much. They are in debt, with very little saved. Two out of every three retirees today are entering retirement with very little saved and large debt loads, usually in the form of a personal mortgage or line of credit. So, what happened?

It didn't happen overnight, it happens over years. It took us time to become desensitized to money due to growing expenses that demanded more of our attention. We began the cycle of larger homes with higher taxes and utilities, children, cars, and status-symbol purchases that we believed improved our lives. We found ourselves working more and rationalizing purchases that were more wants than needs for instant gratification. We all do it. The more money you make, the more money you spend.

Even with all the modern conveniences, it seems we have made our lives more complicated, and have changed from savers to spenders, with an attitude of entitlement. Easy credit from the banks fuelled this national need. We figured that, with the rates being so low, "Ah, why not? I work hard. Why can't I have it?" The banks agreed and gave us more credit, and our debt kept growing. Now what?

When you retire, you need to be debt-free and have a comfortable savings portfolio that meets the lifestyle you anticipate. Most people will not want to lower their standard of living in retirement from what they have become accustomed to. That said, if you are living above your means now in your working years, how do you expect to do this when you are retired with less income? If you are able to develop a new, financially responsible lifestyle to eliminate your debt and save more, it will be easy for you to enjoy your dream plans in retirement.

Fixing your personal finances not only wipes out your debt, but it can fix almost everything else in your life. Once you are on the road to repairing your economic future, I guarantee that all aspects of your life will become better.

It's interesting how much money, or the lack of money, is tied to our personal well-being. Worry about debt and your future can create a sour attitude and can infect your work and home life. It is one of the major contributors toward stress that can undermine your personal and professional life, and many couples today find that they argue more and more about money or even divorce over their financial problems.

Overspending is somewhat like overeating. We rationalize one more cookie or our last supper before a new diet on Monday, just as we rationalize a family holiday on credit. We feel that we really need the vacation and, what's more, we also feel we deserve to have this time for ourselves and our family. When we return from vacation to get the bill, and pay off the credit card with funds from our line of credit, we feel totally defeated again. This has to end if there is to be a wealthy future. You need to put your lifestyle on a diet.

It won't be easy, but nothing important or worthwhile is ever easy. Once you get your budget down to a lean, mean working machine, I guarantee you will be happier. Things will change. Every facet of your life will get better. It works. It's that simple.

ESTABLISHING YOUR CORE

LET'S BEGIN BY GETTING HONEST WITH YOURSELF. THE REASON WHY YOU are not wealthy is you are not willing to do the things to make yourself wealthy. Remember the diet. We want to create a trimmed-down lifestyle that you can easily move through the years with into retirement. We want a lean, workable plan that stays fit and doesn't get bogged down by debt that makes our future so unhealthy. So, let's get started and trim the fat from your budget!

You must be able to live within your means and save every month. The simple structure to your personal net worth is to increase your assets, decrease your liabilities, and establish an investment or savings plan. Plain and simple: you need to build a CORE plan and establish a foundation you can work on. Once your CORE is set up, you can then explore other ways to enhance your wealth, such as investment properties and the stock market.

For most, this exercise might be quite easy, with only minor changes needed to ensure their plan is on track. Some may need to make drastic changes, while others will learn new habits and become better savers. To reach your goals, it is necessary to understand where you are today, where you want to be in the future, and how you will make your plan to get there. Here are the basic steps you need when setting up your CORE plan.

FIVE STEPS TO ESTABLISHING YOUR CORE PLAN

STEP 1: DEBT ELIMINATION

The first step is to eliminate all your outstanding debt other than your mortgage. The easiest method to do this is to consolidate high-interest loans into a new mortgage to capture a lower rate and increase monthly cash flow. This consolidation should be viewed as a one-time transaction to put you on the right road to a debt-free lifestyle. I know I mentioned that you must stop the cycle of refinancing into your mortgage, and if you choose to do this again, please ensure this will be the last time. If, however, you still have outstanding debt after consolidating or were not able to refinance, you will need to tackle one liability at a time and systematically work at paying it off.

The easiest way to do this is to make a list of all your outstanding debt that you wish to eliminate. Pick the one you are going to concentrate on and put as much as you can down on this debt every month, while paying only the minimum payments on the other loans. Once this debt is paid, then move to the next one, repeating the process of paying down one and maintaining the others with only minimum payments. Once all the debt is paid, you can use these new-found funds to start a savings program toward investing. This is when you will stop feeling helpless. Be sure to avoid the tendency to sugar-coat your finances or make excuses to flee from finally resolving your debt. You need to take action, get out of the victim mentality, and start creating certainty and options for your future. It is in the reach of every person to become financially comfortable.

STEP 2: MORTGAGE AMORTIZATION SHOULD
MATCH THE YEARS LEFT TO YOUR RETIREMENT

Set your amortization on your mortgage to match the years you have left until you turn sixty-five. For example, if you are now forty-five, the amortization on your mortgage should be twenty years. All other properties, with the exception of rental properties, should be amortized the same way. This includes vacation homes and cottages.

Most likely your cash flow will improve if you refinance your debt, but always remember not to extend your amortization past your sixty-fifth birthday. It might increase your monthly mortgage payment, but it mostly likely will be less than you were paying before the consolidation. Be smart and plan for the future. Start making decisions based on the bigger picture. See each step you need to take to reach your goals. Keep pushing forward, and always consider your long-term plan.

If you really want a recreational property but can't afford it, consider buying with a relative or good friend. You might find that sharing the monthly expenses, maintenance, and carrying costs is better with someone else. It is a big responsibility to look after more than one home, and having a partner can alleviate some of these chores and help you decide if having a second property on your own is really something you want to entertain in the future. Over time, the co-owners will reap the benefits of the increased value of the investment and can either buy each other out or sell and split the profits.

STEP 3: USE A DAILY CASH JOURNAL AND
FINANCE TRACKER

Use a daily Cash Journal and Finance Tracker to control your expenditures. These are easy tools to help you control your spending and find ways to cut back on the unnecessary costs that drain your monthly income. An example of a Finance Tracker and how to use it follows this section. Please review the Tracker, as it will definitely help you understand where your money is going on a monthly basis. It is a good idea to track for at least six to eight weeks. This is where you will determine if you can live on your income. It is like portion-controlling your expenses.

Today, lifestyles are more expensive than ever, and we seem to have lost the ability to save, to do without, or to wait for things we want. Unfortunately, our society has become obsessed with instant gratification. In order for you to retire wealthy, you need to separate yourself from the others, and take comfort in knowing you are going to be richer than your neighbours.

Always remember that stress comes when you take on too much, accumulate too fast, and make purchases without establishing your CORE wealth. If your current lifestyle is higher than your income and you are regularly reaching for credit, you have only two choices to make: downsize or increase your cash flow. You can't just continue on because of an emotional attachment to things. I see many clients who struggle to maintain their lifestyle with overwhelming debt. Eventually they begin to use debt to make minimum payments on other debt. This is called "kiting." It is when you take a cash advance from a credit card or line of credit to make a minimum payment on another debt or loan. If you are in this situation, you must stop now and begin to make changes. Start thinking like a banker and remove that emotional attachment you have toward your debt. Stop feeling that you must keep it going month to month, telling yourself and believing it will all work out, while getting more in debt with no real end in sight. Those cozy emotional thoughts toward your possessions will quickly disappear with the sobering reality of a sinking net worth and mounting expenses. Most people get consumed by self-doubt, and often will not make the necessary changes to improve their situation. Separate yourself from the new norm in today's society and begin today.

Once you let go, whether it be through downsizing, reworking your expenditures, or moving to a more affordable situation, the stress will dissipate and the feeling of confidence and comfort will begin. Stop limiting yourself and take action. Create new improving financial habits that will wipe out your debt and allow you to reach your goals. Let go of your old habits and create new ones using your Trackers.

STEP 4: DETERMINE YOUR TDS RATIO

TDS stands for total debt servicing ratio, and banks and lenders use it to establish the servicing for increases to your lifestyle. It is a great way for you to determine instantly whether a larger mortgage payment, extra car loan, or additional loan payment can fit into your budget. It is important always to stay within a TDS ratio of 40%. Think of your TDS ratio like a BMI score for a healthy lifestyle, and do not go over the 40% no matter how much you want to. Get your basic CORE plan established before you begin to expand your lifestyle with a larger home, a cottage, and new cars. Today, people go too deep, too early, too fast. Don't make the mistake of being lured in by instant gratification. Once you have established your CORE Plan, it is easy to expand with peace of mind and certainty. Here's how it works.

First, determine your monthly mortgage payment or rent, property taxes, and debt or loan payments. You will also need to take your annual gross income and determine the monthly amount—that is, gross income divided by 12. Typically, banks will include 50% of your condo fees, but we will not be adding this expense in establishing the ratio for your CORE.

- M/R = Monthly mortgage payment or rent payment
- C/L = Monthly credit card or loan payments
- TAX = Monthly property taxes or $0 if you are renting
- GMI = Gross monthly income; annual salary divided by 12

$$M/R + C/L + TAX + \$100 \ / \ GMI = TDS \ x \ 100 \ (\%)$$

Once you have your TDS ratio, you can use it as a benchmark and comfortably know that you can either increase your lifestyle by moving to a larger home or decrease your monthly expenses to lower your ratio below the 40% threshold. Remember not to get mired by short-term setbacks. You must persist with your plan. Use your Trackers together with your TDS ratio. Now let's look at some examples of how best to use the TDS ratio in real-life scenarios.

GRAHAM AND VALERIE

Our first couple live in Ontario and have two older children in their early twenties. They would like to move to a newer home, but are unsure if they can afford it on their incomes. They have updated their 1950s bungalow over the years, and feel that it could sell easily. However, they have accumulated a lot of outstanding debt in addition to their mortgage, and are finding it hard to make a dent in it. Most of their debt was used to upgrade their home and pay for their children's university education. Before they started looking for a newer home, they wanted to determine their current TDS to see if moving up would increase their ratio above 40%. Let's examine their current financial situation. Graham earns $52,000 as an electrician for a large construction company. Valerie earns $26,000 as a customer service manager with a small hotel chain. They currently have a mortgage of $172,000 on a home they have lived in for the past sixteen years and their monthly mortgage payment is $1,970. The value of their house has gone up considerably since they purchased it, but so have all the other homes in their area, which limits what they can spend on their next home. Graham and Valerie have combined credit card debt totalling $27,500 plus a line of credit of $41,000. The minimum monthly payment on their additional debt is $971 and their property taxes are $285 per month. Let's determine their current TDS.

Remember the formula is **M/R + C/L + TAX + \$100 / GMI = TDS x 100 (%)**

- M/R = Monthly mortgage payment or rent payment
- C/L = Monthly credit card or loan payments
- TAX = Monthly property taxes or \$0 if you are renting
- GMI = Gross monthly income. Annual salary divided by 12

M/R \$1,970 + C/L \$971 + TAX \$285 + \$100 / GMI (\$78,000 / 12) \$6,500 = 51.17%

This ratio is very high, and both Graham and Valerie agreed it was getting harder to make ends meet every month with their current commitments. That being said, we wanted to see if making a change could reduce this ratio to the 40% requirement, so we decided to go a little deeper with this situation. When you are calculating your own TDS, please ensure you review every detail of your current finances to determine if making simple changes could lower your ratio. When we looked at Graham and Valerie's credit card debt, we noticed that it was not declining. Only minimum payments were being made, which, if continued over time, eventually would affect their credit bureau scores and lower their ranking with lenders. The interest on their revolving debt was over 19% and their mortgage rate, at 4.95%, was also too high by current standards.

When working out their solution, we wanted to determine if moving would indeed improve their situation. Valerie was tired of living in their neighbourhood, and wanted to move to a newer area closer to work to reduce her commute. She currently took the bus to work, and they wanted to move to an area where she could walk to work every day. They conservatively estimated that they could sell their home for \$375,000, and would like to purchase for a maximum of \$480,000. Let's see what their new TDS would be.

If they sold their house for $375,000, it would be necessary to determine how much money they would have for their new purchase after all expenses. We would pay out their current mortgage, including the fees/penalty, and also eliminate their credit card and credit line debt. To cover all closing costs on their estimated purchase, we would also deduct the land transfer costs and legal fees. Here is how we calculated the surplus from their anticipated sale.

$375,000	Estimated sale of current residence
(179,380)	Less mortgage + fees and penalty
(19,068)	Less real estate fee at 4.5% + 13% HST
(2,400)	Less legal fees (estimated $1,500 to sell + $1,200 to purchase)
(6,075)	Less Ontario land transfer tax on purchase price of $480,000
(27,500)	Less credit card debt paid and closed
(41,000)	Less line of credit paid and closed
$99,577	Funds from sale

To purchase a home for $480,000 with a conventional mortgage, Graham and Valerie would need to put down 20%, or $96,000, which we determined they would have from their sale. A new mortgage for $384,000 amortized over twenty years would have a monthly payment of $2,126. We chose a twenty-year amortization since Graham was the eldest of the two at forty-five and we would want this debt to be paid off by the time he retired at sixty-five. New monthly taxes would be $310. Let's look at their new TDS ratio.

The formula is **M/R + C/L + TAX + $100 / GMI = TDS x 100 (%)**

- M/R = Monthly mortgage payment or rent payment
- C/L = Monthly credit card or loan payments

- TAX = Monthly property taxes or $0 if you are renting
- GMI = Gross monthly income. Annual salary divided by 12

$$M/R \ \$2,126 + C/L \ \$0 + TAX \ \$310 + \$100 \ / \ GMI \ (\$78,000 \ / \ 12)$$
$$\$6,500 = 39.02\%$$

Graham and Valerie wanted to move to another home, and our financial advice was to do so. By upgrading their home, they not only improved their lifestyle with a more modern home but they single-handily eliminated their debt, lowered the high interest costs on a new mortgage, and reduced their TDS ratio to within guidelines. They no longer live with revolving debt that had once become such a tremendous stress and burden to their lifestyle. Now they have a newer home that mostly likely will increase in value more than their previous home, ultimately increasing their overall net worth by retirement. Well done.

Let's look at another example.

GUY AND YVONNE

Guy and Yvonne are thinking of purchasing a recreational property, and have decided to buy a cottage. Yvonne recently received an inheritance of $50,000 from her grandmother, and wants to use these funds as the down payment on the purchase. The cottage is on a very small lake and could be purchased for $230,000. Guy and Yvonne want to put down only 20% as a deposit and plan to get a mortgage for the balance.

Here is how we estimated their new mortgage.

$230,000	Purchase price of cottage
(46,000)	Less 20% deposit
$184,000	**New mortgage**

In addition to the $46,000 down payment, this couple would have to pay legal fees estimated at $750 and the land transfer tax of $2,050 for the province of Quebec. It is a good idea also to budget for additional costs such as home inspection, septic and water testing, land surveying, etc.

To determine their new TDS, we need to look at their current financial commitments and add the monthly cottage expenses. Guy earns $95,000 as an engineer and Yvonne makes $72,000 as a human resources manager at a mid-sized manufacturing company. They currently have a mortgage of $320,000, with a monthly payment of $2,195, and their property taxes are $420 per month. Yvonne has approximately $5,000 in credit card debt and Guy has a car payment of $690 per month. Let's look at their current TDS and how it will change with the purchase of their recreational property.

The formula is **M/R + C/L + TAX + $100 / GMI = TDS x 100(%)**

- M/R = Monthly mortgage payment or rent payment
- C/L = Monthly credit card or loan payments
- TAX = Monthly property taxes or $0 if you are renting
- GMI = Gross monthly income. Annual salary divided by 12

M/R $2,195 + C/L $785 + TAX $420 + $100 / GMI ($167,000 / 12) $13,916 = 25.15%

Their current TDS is 25.15%, well within guidelines. Here is how we worked out their new TDS ratio for the cottage purchase. The new mortgage payment would be $1,147 and property taxes $383.

M/R ($2,195 + $1,147) + C/L $785 + TAX ($420 + $383) + $200 / GMI $13,916 = 36.87%

Clearly, Guy and Yvonne earn enough to purchase this second property, and can feel confident that they will have no trouble qualifying for this purchase. As long as they continue to keep their credit card debt low, they can easily work at paying off their mortgages by retirement and have the added bonus of two increasing assets that will grow their net worth over time.

A word of caution here when thinking of buying a cottage or cabin as a second residence. Canadian banks have many new restrictions on recreational use properties, and you will want to ensure the property you wish to purchase will indeed qualify for a mortgage. Banks have set up new standard guidelines to mitigate risk, and it is a good idea to have your lender appraise the property (at their cost) before you waive your financing conditions at the time of purchase. If your chosen cottage has any one of the features in the list below, it will be declined by the big banks and will need to be underwritten by a secondary lender. It is also possible that the purchase might not even qualify, and therefore you might have to restructure your primary residence to increase an already existing mortgage in an effort to cover the cottage purchase. Here are some of the features that might cause lenders to decline your request for financing:

- property is located on rented land (99-year deed);
- property is a mobile home or trailer;
- no running water, no septic system;
- no indoor plumbing, bathroom, etc.;
- no basement, full or partial;
- no permanent heat source, the property must have a furnace;
- no year-round access;
- seasonal home only, not insulated, etc.;
- no road access to residence.

Determining your TDS is very easy and acts as a non-discriminatory "tell it like it is" ratio for anyone wanting to ensure their current financial situation is on the right track. Of course, if you are living month to month and constantly reaching for credit to supplement living expenses, you already know that your TDS will be over 40%. Unfortunately, there are far too many situations where well-meaning, good people have got into financial trouble. I have seen countless examples of seasoned brokers and small lenders twisting a deal to make it fit the banking matrix, ultimately overextending a new client who really never should have been qualified and, of course, is now unable to manage their debt. Whether you are planning to buy a second property, move to a larger home, purchase a new car, or even restructure your debt to lower your ranking, you should always adhere to the 40% benchmark. It is very lenient, and there should be no reason why you need to live over this percentage.

Right now, work out your own TDS ratio and play with the monthly amounts. Don't just do it because you need to, do it because you want to. Concentrate on the small steps toward your future, rather than staying cemented in the past. Remember, everyone has the ability to retire wealthy. But it isn't for slackers; you have to work at it. Stay within the 40% and you will get there. Guaranteed.

STEP 5: EXPLORE WAYS TO INCREASE YOUR WEALTH

Once your CORE finances are in order and you have no credit card debt, begin exploring ways to save with other investment initiatives to supplement your retirement. If you are considering a move to a larger home, buying a recreational property, or even starting a new career or business venture, make sure to plan for all expenditures. Having your CORE finances in order will ensure your foundation for achievement is well grounded, and will allow you to concentrate or your future success without the worry of monetary setbacks.

Research your employer and consider contributing to a company pension or savings plan. Start saving systematically and consider having a set amount deducted from your income at source. This will make it easier to budget while creating a savings program in a secure investment portfolio. I'll discuss later how to use the "bucket concept" in the chapter on retirement dreaming. Here, I'll show you how to plan your own timeline and customize your financial goals based on your current budget and projected future savings. You will need to develop three distinct savings buckets tailored to your future plans—for example, honeymoon fund + retirement fund + long-term pension fund. Don't worry too much about this now. All the steps, techniques, and methods on how to retire wealthy are here for you to learn, and I have no doubt that you will become debt-free and financially secure.

Everyone needs an easy to maintain and realistic long-term strategy to become wealthy, but our natural instinct is to keep doing what we have always done and what is familiar. I want you to consider treating your finances like a business. Remember, companies that expand too fast and find that they are not making enough money to pay for their expenditures will cut their losses and make changes. The company doesn't die; it just goes in another direction and becomes profitable again.

Become the CEO of your financial future. You might even want to create your own corporate vision statement, which articulates your dream lifestyle today and in the future. It is always easier to plan for the future if you have a picture or plan of where you want to be. Make the hard decisions to keep your budget and future in business. Refuse to consider failure and don't depend on anyone else. Only you can create a successful lifestyle plan, customized for you and your family. You can do it. Use your Trackers, dissolve your debt, and begin saving. Always make the small steps toward learning new habits and improving your life.

THE
CASH
TRACKER

THE CASH TRACKER IS A SIMPLE JOURNAL TO KEEP TRACK OF ALL FUNDS flowing in and out of your account. Here, you will budget for all the expenses you have day to day against your income and savings. It is always a good idea to have one main bank account when budgeting with your journal. If you have multiple accounts, you might want to have a separate journal for each to make it easier to monitor all transactions.

I once went to an art show and watched a very skilled artist using a potter's wheel to craft a large bowl. As the wheel spun, he made a small dent in the side of the bowl, which created deep ridges. Sometimes the bowl had to be thrown away, and he started again. As I watched the artist, I was struck by how our finances are so similar to this concept. As long as we keep our finances on track, we can create a great future for ourselves, but when we put a dent in our budget or overextend too much, the plan collapses and needs to be started again. It will be necessary to put the brakes on any discretionary spending and perhaps stop indulging in costly wants and must-haves.

Tracking expenses automatically forces you to re-evaluate the way you spend money, and allows you to see first-hand exactly where your hard-earned income is going. You will be surprised at how consciously involved you will become in tracking your daily finances. I guarantee, once you begin, you will be more motivated to pay down debt and eliminate high-interest charges and monthly carrying costs.

Don't worry if you have a lot of debt or your finances are a mess. Forgive yourself and get on with it. Set up a plan to learn new habits and become better. Don't settle for less. Here, we begin Step 1 of your CORE Plan and tackle one debt at a time. Once one debt has successfully been paid off, duplicate the action, and keep doing it until all debts are eliminated. You can then begin to save. Remember, there is no shortcut. Money is emotional. The reality is, everyone should be tracking, and now that you are, you are on the road to successful money management. Good for you!

This is an example of how you will use your journal.

CASH TRACKER

Bank Account: _____

DATE	DESCRIPTION	CASH IN	CASH OUT	BALANCE
June 1	Bank account balance			$982.02
June 3	Paycheque deposited	$1,253.79		$2,235.81
June 3	Cable bill		$43.92	$2,191.89
June 3	Phone bill		$28.41	$2,163.48
June 3	Credit card payment		$385.20	$1,778.28
June 4	Groceries		$189.36	$1,588.92
June 5	Rent		$850.00	$738.92
June 6	Birthday gift money	$100.00		$838.92

CASH TRACKER

Bank Account: _____

DATE	DESCRIPTION	CASH IN	CASH OUT	BALANCE

THE FINANCE TRACKER

THIS TRACKER IS DESIGNED TO HELP YOU SEE ALL YOUR MONTHLY expenses at a glance. Here, we will sort out the mandatory expenses and show areas that can be eliminated to create greater cash flow. You will easily be able to determine your monthly costs and develop new strategies and alternatives to resist the urge to overspend. We want you to trim down any costly expenses that make your budget too fat and overweight. Together with your daily Cash Tracker, we can create a tight, lean, portion-controlled budget.

Creating a new budget is not easy. It is best to work on your Tracker with your partner, spouse, or roommate. Having someone else to be accountable to will help keep you on track. Once you start planning and tracking your expenditures, you will move from powerless to powerful. Don't be a victim of your own unwillingness to make changes for the better. You can do it!

HOW TO USE YOUR FINANCE TRACKER

First, let's use four coloured pens: blue, green, yellow/orange, and red. If you have highlighter pens or markers, they are good, too.

To start, fill out all your income in the box for monthly sources of income. Use your blue marker or pen to show all the money you acquire every month.

Next, use your green pen—because green means GO— and fill in all the monthly expenses that are considered mandatory.

Now let's switch to your yellow/orange pen, because I want you to be aware that these expenses should be treated in a more cautious and conservative manner. This is where you will need to decide whether these expenses can be reduced, reworked, or perhaps even eliminated to find additional available funds month to month. Groceries are included in this group because I want you to see if you can reduce your monthly amount by shopping at less expensive stores or perhaps by cutting back on high-priced items.

Fill in the last boxes with your red pen/marker. Red means STOP. These are expenses you should seriously consider removing from your budget altogether unless you can justify them to your Tracker partner. Try doing things for yourself, rather than hiring a service. Read over the "Ways to Save" section and find new ways to change old, expensive habits. Here are some examples:

- Have a student, rather than an expensive service, mow your lawn.
- Pack your lunch instead of buying out every day while at work.
- Cut out the daily specialty coffee beverages; consider this a treat on special occasions only.
- Stop the spontaneous purchases for children, pets, and yourself. Ask yourself, "Do I really need to buy this?"

Once all your amounts are in the correct boxes, it will be easy for you to evaluate your expenditures and find ways to cut back and save more. A simple calculation will show how much disposable income is left over every month.

Income - **Mandatory Expenses** - **Discretionary Expenses**= $_____
 (blue)   **(green)**   **(yellow/orange)**

CONGRATULATIONS ON FINDING MORE INCOME!

Remember, this extra income should be used to pay down debts or put toward a new savings plan.

MONTHLY SOURCES OF INCOME (BLUE)

Salary		Royalty income	
Bonuses/commissions		Child support	
Net self-employment		OAS/GIS	
Net rental income		CPP/QPP	
Alimony		Company pension	
Dividend income		LRIF/LIF/PRIF income	
Interest income		RRIF income	
Capital gains income		Trust or annuity income	

Total Monthly Income = $ _____

MONTHLY EXPENSES (GREEN)

Rent or mortgage payment		Condo fees	
Hydro		Water/sewer	
House/apartment insurance		Gas/propane/heating	
Auto registration/licence		Property taxes	
Car insurance		CPP/QPP premiums	
Debt-1 (min. payment + 10%)		Payroll deductions	
Debt-2 (min. payment + 10%)		Alimony payments	
Debt-3 (min. payment + 10%)		Child support payment	
Debt-4 (min. payment + 10%)		RSP loan repayments	
Debt-5 (min. payment + 10%)		Student loans	
Debt-6 (min. payment + 10%)		Miscellaneous:	
Debt-7 (min. payment + 10%)		Miscellaneous:	
Debt-8 (min. payment + 10%)		Miscellaneous:	

Total Monthly Expenses = $ _____

MONTHLY EXPENSES (YELLOW/ORANGE)

Home telephone		Groceries	
Cellular telephone		Specialty food purchases	
Babysitting/child care		Automotive gas/fuel	
Home security		Car repairs and oil changes	
Cable TV		Auto lease/finance payment	
Clothing		Parking	
Gifts		Public transportation	
Hair salon/barber		Medical insurance	
Books/music		Prescription drugs	
Dependant home care		Dental expenses	
Veterinarian services		Over-the-counter drugs	
Magazine/newspapers		Banking fees	
Internet services		Children's extra curricular activities	
Other:		Miscellaneous:	
Other:		Miscellaneous:	

Total Monthly Expenses = $ _____

MONTHLY EXPENSES (RED)

Dry cleaning		Alcohol/tobacco	
Dining out		Movie rentals	
House cleaning services		Movie/concerts/shows	
Catered meal services		Lottery tickets/gambling	
Handyman services		Vacation, air fare	
Home repairs/ maintenance		Vacation, accommodations	
Garden supplies		Vacation, food	
Pet boarding		Vacation, house/pet sitter	
Pet-walking services		Vacation, travel insurance	
Pet expenses		Vacation, souvenirs	
Miscellaneous spending		Vacation, rental car	
Health club dues		Vacation, cottage rental	
Other membership dues		Pool cleaning/services	
User fees		Lawn care services	
Sports equipment		Snow removal services	

Team dues		Personal grooming services	
Toys/child gear		Massage/spa services	
Spontaneous purchases for kids		Buying lunches out	
Spontaneous purchases for personal use		Specialty coffee beverages	
Expensive hobbies, fees, memberships, etc.		Expensive supplies for hobbies	
Other:		Miscellaneous:	
Other:		Miscellaneous:	

Total Monthly Expenses = $ _____ .

CLIENT STORIES:

How to Eliminate Debt before Retirement

DEBT. WHAT CAN I SAY? WE ALL HAVE IT. TODAY IS NOT THE SAME AS IT was for our parents. In the 1960s and '70s, lifestyles were cheaper, houses were less expensive, and we certainly did not have the vast selection of products that we do today. Our insatiable need for bigger and better has provided a booming market for businesses, creating slick, enticing ads that draw us in to spend more. In the past, most couples had paid off their mortgages by their late forties. Today, the average couple at age forty-six is nowhere near paying off their mortgage, let alone their other mounting debt in the form of credit cards and personal lines of credit. So, what should we do?

More than any other time in history, we are living in a world flooded with information, yet we are still starved for valuable, customized knowledge. No one wants to share their ideas and stories of how they created wealth. Most of us keep our finances very private, and suffer in silence with the anxiety and stress of mounting debt. The uncertainty of our own future security in retirement can be a sobering thought as we near the end of our working career.

If you are reading this book, you are probably determined not to be one of the statistics that now show that two out of every three couples entering retirement have a high debt load. Sometimes, all that is needed is simply to redirect funds into more conservative saving habits and stop the impulse purchases. Other times, more drastic measures need to be made to devise proper debt-elimination strategies and stop the high interest charges eating away your hard-earned monthly income. As well, we must begin to accept that government programs by themselves are just not enough to fund our future retirement. Now, with the new economic landscape, we might need to consider changing our outlook on retirement and, unfortunately, working until sixty or sixty-five might not be enough. Working longer is now becoming commonplace, as many find that they have just not saved enough.

Let's begin with stories of everyday people like you who have shared their stories of success and change to better their financial futures. From single parents or divorced couples starting over to self-made business owners and dual-income families living paycheque to paycheque, all have made money through different techniques. All of these stories are very different, and will offer you ways to make changes in your own financial life to help ensure that you get to retirement debt-free and wealthy. Become inspired, learn some new money-management techniques, and see how to borrow wisely from the banks. Start to take control of your financial future. You can do it, too!

Finally, all the secrets are out in the open. You owe it to yourself to discover the ways to become wealthy.

Good luck!

LEVERAGE LENDING TO PAY OFF A MORTGAGE: LAURIE AND PAT

I first met Laurie and Pat about twelve years ago when I helped them with their mortgage on the purchase of a new home. They were moving to a much larger home in the same town. At the time, we were able to consolidate all their additional debt from the sale proceeds. They had three young children, and both had a good income. A typical family, working hard and trying to get ahead. Many couples, during their working years, try to accumulate savings and assets to increase net worth, but simply saving up the entire purchase price of a family home today is virtually impossible. The use of credit is a valuable tool for creating wealth, but it can be debilitating when nearing retirement, and these clients knew they needed to create a plan to pay down their mortgage.

Unfortunately, life nowadays is quite expensive, and it is typical to have a large mortgage, car loans, and credit card debt. With the increased demands of a lifestyle with three active kids, Laurie and Pat were feeling the financial squeeze. Pat had recently been laid off from his $95,000 senior management position with the company to which he had devoted the last twenty years of his career. This was an emotional and financial blow to the family, and once the dust settled, Pat decided to start a small business in the same field with another co-worker who had also been let go. They started an import company, and used their compensation packages to fund the venture. Laurie continued to work full time, earning $62,000 per year. Their mortgage was $398,000, and they had one daughter away at university and two others still at home in high school. Living primarily on Laurie's income, their debt was mounting; however, Pat was able to make about $32,000 in his first year. Not bad for starting his own business, but still much lower than he was used to making.

They had $45,300 on their line of credit and another $25,600 spread across three credit cards. They had also co-signed for their eldest daughter's school loan, and were supporting her with $450 per month toward lodging and food while away at university. They did not have a car loan, but were thinking of getting one to replace a vehicle that now had over 260,000 miles on it. They also wanted to do some home repairs, and were planning on using the deferred payment options through a local hardware store. They had $14,500 in an investment and $31,000 in a savings account. Their home was worth about $800,000. Laurie was fifty-two and had a good pension plan, so she intended to continue with the same employer until she retired. Pat was fifty-six and did not have a pension. He was now self-employed, and had liquidated any hope of a pension allowance when he cashed in his employee savings plan along with his severance package for the new business venture.

When we went through their finances and completed a financial plan, it was obvious that they would not be ready for the planned retirement in nine years, when Pat would turn sixty-five. Pat was confident that his new business would rescue their financial situation, but Laurie was not so sure. The continuous pressure on Pat to grow his business and make more money was causing him to take on more risk, and the strain on their relationship was escalating. Their current net worth was $376,600, mainly based on the value of their home. If the market were to change and house prices were to go down, their net worth would decline accordingly. With no real savings and mounting debt, something had to change.

While interest rates were low, we could use a leverage lending concept to help pay down their mortgage faster and reduce anticipated higher interest costs should the rates rise in the future. It was possible to turn things around completely, but the solution we proposed entailed a lot of lifestyle changes. With the added expenses of two other children soon to be entering college or university and an increasing debt load, it was obvious that this couple needed to do something. This is quite a typical situation. Most people today are so highly leveraged with current debt, that if interest rates were to rise on mortgages, the effects on some families would be catastrophic. Like Laurie and Pat, most people are leaving themselves extremely vulnerable to the risk of rising interest rates, and are not making any attempts to pay down debt. Let's look at what would happen if rates were to rise only two or three percentage points in the coming years.

$398,000 **Current mortgage at 2.89%, amortized over 23 years =**
$1,990 per month
Total interest paid over 5 years = $54,316
Balance after 5 years = $332,905
Current remaining amortization = 18 years
$332,905 **Renewal at higher rate of 5.39% (2.5% increase), amortized**
over 18 years
= $2,450 per month
Total interest paid over next 5 years = $82,520
Balance after 5 years = $275,380

With an increase in rates, even on the lower mortgage amount, the interest paid over a five-year term has now increased by 52% and the monthly payment increased by 24%. With only nine years to their projected retirement, this couple would certainly not be debt-free, but would walk into retirement, like most, with outstanding debt in the form of a mortgage. They might be forced to sell their home to pay off the mortgage, and let's hope that the housing market has not gone down when they plan to do so.

Bottom line, these clients need to pay down or at least try to get rid of their debt and build a savings portfolio. Leaving your future security in the hands of a new business venture, with little time left for recovery if it doesn't work out, is extremely risky.

SO WHAT DID THEY DO?

There are many banking products available today that offer flexibility from the standard mortgage format. Laurie and Pat had good credit, and could take advantage of new products, now available from almost all lenders, in the form of a home equity line of credit (HELOC) or a collateral charge. These products change the landscape of a typical mortgage offering, and now allow customers to divide their equity into two or more segments with a variety of options. A HELOC gives clients a mortgage segment and a line of credit portion that use the equity built up in the home. A collateral charge is very similar to a HELOC, but allows for more division of equity. Most collateral charges will offer five or more segments to provide both a better platform for structuring a financial plan and clarity when dividing debt and entertaining investment options.

Here, we should pause to provide some clarity of our own on the alternative products the big banks are now offering their clients. To acquire more market share, the banks have designed products that are more flexible and give greater choice and freedom than the standard mortgage to which we have all become accustomed.

WHAT IS A HELOC?

All the big Canadian banks have some form of homeowner line of credit that typically can be placed into only two segments. One segment can be a conventional mortgage, variable or fixed; the other segment is a secured line of credit. You can borrow up to 80% of the value of your residence, but if your mortgage portion is too low or if you only wish to have a line of credit, you will be able to borrow only up to 65% loan-to-value. This is a federal government–mandated stipulation on all Canadian lenders to ensure lines of credit are kept below the 65% threshold. Basically, once you pay off your mortgage, you can use your HELOC as a secured open line of credit and pay interest only on any balance outstanding.

WHAT IS A COLLATERAL CHARGE?

All the big banks now have some form of collateral charge, but their offerings vary, so it is a good idea to review all the details before you jump in. Basically, a collateral charge can be placed for the full 100% value of your property and provides the flexibility to borrow more funds if needed in the future. As a collateral charge is considered to be a lifetime open-lending tool, clients can have multiple loan segments under their plan, which can easily be manipulated. Clients may choose to pay off their loans, set up new loans, or even change the terms, frequency, and amortization of existing loans. This product provides many options for estate and financial planning, and need be registered only once on title.

WHAT IS A REVERSE MORTGAGE?

I am not in favour of reverse mortgages, and do not recommend them. If you are entertaining getting one, I invite you to call me first. Still, it's good to know what they are. A reverse mortgage is generally offered to a client over age fifty-five, and typically is available only through small, independent brokerages. With this type of product, homeowners can borrow 50–55% of their equity, which is typically paid out in a lump sum. Once you have signed for the reverse mortgage, you will not have to make any payments or repay the loan for as long as you live in your home. Upon your death, however, the loan, payments, and "compounded" interest will be payable. Depending how long you lived in your home, this could add up to the entire value of your residence when the loan is finally called, ultimately leaving nothing for your heirs. Due to continuous rising inflation and the constant fluctuation of the Canadian dollar, we regularly advise clients to seek other alternatives for equity takeouts. I have often heard bankers say that reverse mortgages are easier to acquire and better than conventional secured lines of credit. This is not true. Talk to your advisor and do your homework before you sign over your home.

LET'S NOW GO BACK TO LOOK AT LAURIE AND PAT'S SOLUTION.
The appraised value of Laurie and Pat's home was $800,000, which means that, under a HELOC or collateral charge, they would be able to access 80%, or $640,000. We chose to use the collateral charge because we wanted the multiple segments to isolate their mortgage, debt, and a new leverage loan segment.

One of the first things we needed to address was Pat's business venture. We talked at great length about his business and how he was considering expanding with a third partner, allowing him more time. Pat then decided to return to his old employer, who now wanted him back, and would continue with his new business on the side, part time. His employment income would be lower, at $89,000, but it would now include a company car. This made it very easy to qualify Laurie and Pat, with their current financial institution, for our chosen lending product.

We were able to keep their mortgage rate on the mortgage segment portion of their new collateral charge, which allowed us to take advantage of a very low interest rate for the balance of the four-year term. The line of credit and balances on their credit cards were added together to form another segment that had a fixed monthly payment and an amortization to match Pat's goal for retirement in nine years. By keeping this debt separate and refusing to amalgamate it into the mortgage, we could ensure the debt would be eliminated quickly, without any added interest charges from compounding in a mortgage. We also set up a leverage loan with a fixed rate and term of four years to match the mortgage segment. Finally, we changed all the payments from monthly to weekly to further minimize interest charges. Here is what it looked like.

<u>Collateral charge = $640,000</u>
<u>Segment 1:</u>
$398,000 mortgage at 2.89%, 23-year amortization = $455/week

<u>Segment 2:</u>
$71,000 debt at 3.00%, 9-year amortization = $173/week
<u>Segment 3:</u>
$170,000 leverage loan, fixed rate 3%, 25-year amortization = $185/week
<u>Segment 4:</u>
$1,000 line of credit limit with $0 balance (not to be used)

Most people dismiss leverage lending because they really do not understand the power of compounding. In the current interest rate market of low borrowing rates, you can use this technique and save thousands of dollars. This technique is common practice with affluent clients, and is often referred to as the "monetization" of money, usually done with a minimum of a million dollars invested.

WHAT IS MONETIZATION?

Monetization means to covert, change, or exchange money. In banking terms, this is when you invest money in a secured asset or platform over a set period of time to realize a guaranteed gain when you cash out. Since the international financial crisis of 2008, many investment strategies have continuously moved in and out of favour with advisors and fund managers, but the method of monetization, used in a disciplined strategy, has never underperformed. It is still highly favoured by top asset managers who are seeking qualitative growth and quantitative returns for their large portfolio funds. Let's see how it worked out for Laurie and Pat.

For this couple, the simplified monetization solution created a forced savings plan under a very controlled situation. To reduce risk, you must ensure that the loan rate is secured for a fixed term that matches the security you are using with the investment. For these clients, we wanted to eliminate almost all risk, so we chose a triple-A institutional compounding strip bond with a short duration to match the loan. The bond rate was 5.1363% and was locked in for four years. The benefit of leverage lending is that the interest paid on the loan can be used as a tax write-off, and is necessary to offset the income tax you will pay on the gains. Since Pat's income is the highest, he will be able to use this loan to further reduce his marginal tax rate and lower his overall income tax.

Most people think they can achieve the same results just by doubling up their mortgage payments by the same amount, but here you will see what our wealthy clients have known all along: the power of compounding is truly magical. It is similar to the same concept of how banks calculate their mortgages, only in reverse. Let's examine the difference between simply increasing their weekly payments on their mortgage versus using the power of the leverage lending concept.

In segment one, Pat and Laurie have the rate secured for another four years at 2.89%, and when it is up for renewal the balance will be $345,965. If they were to increase their weekly payment by $185 and not leverage lend, they could expect the balance to be $305,209. Pretty impressive, right? This is a savings of $40,756 simply by increasing their weekly payments. Now let's look at the leverage lending concept.

Because Laurie had $30,000 in a cash savings account, we were able to add this to the $170,000 we borrowed, making our total institutional bond purchase $200,000. You should use nonregistered funds or cash for this concept to take advantage of the tax incentive. This process cannot be used with registered investments such as RRSPs since they do not provide a tax write-off and are taxed heavily when cashed out—I will talk about using compounding strip bonds and leverage lending for RRSPs in the chapter on Retirement Dreaming. For this scenario, we wanted all investments to be nonregistered.

The leverage payment was the same, at $185 per week, and we made sure this was a principal-plus-interest payment for the loan. At the end of the four years, the bond will cash out at $256,940, while the couple still enjoy the tax savings every year by writing off the interest payments on the loan. For the leverage loan in segment three, the amount outstanding to be paid out will be $150,434 on the original $170,000 borrowed. We will also need to give back the $30,000 we used from Laurie's cash fund.

Here is how we calculated the gain.

$256,940	**Cashing out the bond after four years**
(150,434)	**Less outstanding balance to be paid off on segment 3**
(30,000)	**Less nonregistered funds returned to Laurie**
	(no loss of funds, secured capital, and returned)
$76,506	**Available funds to put down on mortgage as lump sum**

The segment 1 mortgage balance at renewal would be $345,965, and before we renew again for another term, we will put down the lump sum of $76,506, adjusting the balance to $269,459. When comparing this balance with the $305,209 balance from increasing only the mortgage payments, we now understand the power of the compounding leverage loan, which generates an extra $35,750 in only four years.

FORTY-EIGHT MONTHS LATER

When we reviewed Laurie and Pat's finances four years later, their mortgage was just under $270,000. They had used the leverage lending model and were very happy about reducing their mortgage by $128,000 in such a short time. Of course, this took a lot of compromise and commitment by both of them to keep up with their weekly payments. Pat's personal business was doing well with his new partners, and he was able to capture approximately $36,000 in dividend income annually from his venture. They were both still working full time, and now all three kids were in university. Segment two, the debt loan, was down to $41,700, and they were determined to maintain their commitment to pay it off in five years. They decided to leverage lend again for the next five years and to keep their payments the same, since they had already budgeted them into their lifestyle. The balance on their mortgage after this new five-year solution would be $52,981, and here is how it was achieved.

<u>Maintained original collateral charge = $640,000</u>
Segment 1:
$269,459 mortgage at 3.00%, 14-year amortization= $453/week
Segment 2:
$41,700 debt at 3.00%, 5-year amortization= $173/week
Segment 3:
$170,000 leverage loan, fixed rate 3%, 25-year amortization = $185/week
Segment 4:
$157,841 available line of credit with $0 balance (not to be used)

Since their mortgage had decreased, there was available room on the line of credit portion of the collateral charge. We could have used these additional funds in our leverage loan; however, the clients did not want to deviate from the original setup, and purchased a $200,000 institutional compounding strip bond in the same manner as before. This bond had a compounded yield of 5.6239% and would mature at $277,760 after five years. Here is how we cashed out their strategy.

$277,760	**Cashing out the bond after five years**
(145,169)	**Less outstanding balance to be paid off on segment 3**
(30,0000)	**Less nonregistered funds returned to Laurie**
	(no loss of funds, secured capital, and returned)
$102,591	**Available funds to put down on mortgage as lump sum**

$185,572	Mortgage renewal at five years
(102,591)	Less lump sum from leverage lend
(30,000)	Less savings funds/Laurie decided to put her savings toward their debt
$52,981	New mortgage balance**

**Pat felt that this was a manageable balance that he could pay off with his business dividend income and did so within two years.

Laurie could count on a pension income of $27,000 at retirement. Pat decided to postpone his retirement age from sixty-five to sixty-eight, still continuing his personal business on the side. Their net worth was mainly tied up in their home; however, once the debt was eliminated, they began increasing their cash savings every month. When Pat turned sixty-eight, they had saved approximately $105,000, and their new net worth was $1,040,000, not including Pat's business partnership.

While I am the first to admit that you must have a separate savings plan for retirement, these clients essentially secured this through paying into Laurie's pension plan and continuing to grow Pat's business. By leverage lending, they easily eliminated all future debt expenses and insulated themselves against the risk of carrying any debt when the rates inevitably increase. They have no worries, and they have successfully created a comfortable retirement life. Pat's partnership in his business can be sold in the future to realize additional funds, and they will probably downsize to a smaller home and capture the equity they worked so hard for.

COACH'S MESSAGE

The reality is that most people don't even recall what their interest rate is on their mortgage nor do they know when it will be paid off. Being absent-minded about your debt will only guarantee future financial hardships. As with the example of Laurie and Pat, the risk of rising rates is one thing, but what about the possibility of job loss? Most people would be in severe jeopardy if either were to occur.

The fact remains that we have been accumulating debt faster and in far greater amounts than our income, and it is no surprise that mortgage debt has vastly increased due to rising house prices. Although we love having low mortgage rates, this low interest rate environment has only helped fuel the overextension of more debt that people can't help getting into. Rising house prices are creating debt levels that many pre-retirees will continue to carry well into retirement for many years. Savvy clients see the low lending rates as an opportunity to provide a tax incentive vehicle to help them reduce nontaxable bad debt through leverage lending and monetization.

Currently, the housing market is still stable with continued projected growth and low interest rates. But when rates increase, will you be ready, or will you be so far in debt that you won't be able to break free? You must always have a plan to eliminate your mortgage before you retire. Living on a reduced fixed income will greatly reduce your ability to pay off a mortgage, let alone handle any increased payments due to higher interest rates.

Remember to follow the steps in establishing your CORE Plan. This will help you create a customized, budget-minded lifestyle. Make sure you consider all smart planning concepts and talk to the professionals. There are many other products and services that can help you eliminate debt and create a sizable savings fund for your future. You owe it to yourself to become more knowledgeable and more involved in your personal finances. Remember that banks have many other products other than traditional fixed or variable mortgages that can help you eliminate debt and create a sizable savings fund for your future. You owe it to yourself to become more knowledgeable and more involved in your personal finances. Do your homework. You will be surprised by what options are open to you to help you reach your goal.

WAITING FOR THE INHERITANCE THAT NEVER CAME: LISA AND JACK

Companies, big or small, are always trying to find ways to tighten up their budgets, and I have had many clients laid off or downsized, subsequently finding themselves in a very difficult financial predicament. If they were lucky enough to be terminated with a severance package, they might need only to mend their broken ego. But if they were fired or walked out, it is hard to know how to continue a family lifestyle filled with financial commitments. Most people believe this could never happen because they either have long tenure with their employer or their position is too important. Don't be so sure. Preparation means ensuring you are prepared for the unexpected. I have seen many well-educated senior executives with years of experience simply let go without warning.

Jack was a senior VP of a mid-sized privately owned company and made $230,000 a year. His wife was a nurse and made $72,000. They had two boys and lived in a modest home in the suburbs worth approximately $550,000. I had known Jack and Lisa for many years, and had refinanced their mortgage many times to consolidate debt and help them invest their savings of $150,000. Jack loved to live large. He had just purchased a new ski boat for over $83,000, which he financed with another monthly payment. A Porsche, motorcycle, and jet ski were some of his other toys. Both his and his wife's cars were leased, and the family went on two vacations every year; down south for the winter and Europe for the summer.

When Jack was fired from his executive position, he was devastated. His severance was very good, and allowed the family to continue its high lifestyle for another twelve months. However, Jack could not find another comparable position that he felt was suitable. Another eighteen months would go by before I saw Lisa and Jack again. Jack had now taken a senior management position close to home that would pay $125,000, almost half of what he was used to earning. By the time we reviewed their finances, it was evident that they were not doing well. Debt was consuming them. Lisa looked very stressed, and was visibly worried about their financial predicament. Jack, on the other hand, was calm and collected, as usual. They had maxed out every credit card, line of credit, and overdraft, while the continuous monthly interest charges quietly ate away at their disposable incomes.

Unfortunately, I was not able to refinance their mortgage and unsecured debt. They simply owed more than they were worth, and the banks would not take the risk. Consolidating debt into a mortgage or loan does not take the debt away; it only groups it together and spreads out the amortization to make the payments smaller and more manageable. If there is too much outstanding credit, lenders will consider the client high risk and will not want to consolidate for fear that the client will either default on the new loan or go out and acquire more debt.

Lisa and Jack had a mortgage of $495,000, a $7,000 overdraft loan, two lines of credit totalling $53,200, credit cards maxed at $62,100, car lease payments, a boat loan, and another consolidation loan for $19,600. The monthly interest was approximately $4,320 just to carry the commitments, and their credit ratings were slowly sinking with the continuous revolving debt load. Their net worth was NEGATIVE –$96,200, with this number going further in the hole each month.

My advice to these clients was to cut their losses and sell all their depreciating assets. I suggested they sell the boat, jet ski, and motorcycle, and cash in their investments to pay down debt. Normally, we would never suggest to clients to liquidate a registered investment. However, Jack had been able to take advantage of the reduction in income tax when he was earning a much larger salary, and now that his income was lower, it would be more advantageous to cash in part of his investment and pay taxes at a lower marginal tax rate. Also, when we compared the return on their investment over the previous year to the amount of interest they paid, it did not make sense to leave the funds in the plan. Only by reducing their debt burden could they hope to refinance with the banks in the future to realize lower rates and ultimately lower monthly payments.

SO WHAT DID THEY DO?

Jack did not want to change his lifestyle no matter how bad the current circumstances were. At fifty-two, he was desperate for an amicable solution, and now realizing that the banks could not help, he went to his parents. Jack's parents were quite well off, with an estimated portfolio of just over $2,000,000. They were great examples of successful savers. They had worked hard, done without, and always saved as much as they could. Jack's mother was a retired teacher and his father a retired insurance agent. Saving diligently every year was a habit they wanted to instil in their only son. Jack, however, viewed their frugality more as a sacrifice and evidence of a neglected childhood. His parents gave him $250,000. Jack used the funds to pay off his immediate debts, and wanted to refinance the balance of his debt in a new mortgage with the banks.

Instead of refinancing into a standard mortgage, Jack chose a secured line of credit on his property. By using a line of credit, he would now be responsible only for the interest payments, unlike a mortgage, which requires a payment of principal plus interest. The only benefit of the line of credit is that the monthly payments are much lower; however, the loan never decreases and the rate is slightly higher to account for risk. Jack's prime objective was to keep the monthly commitments low, and he assured me that he would switch it to a principal-plus-interest payment once he got back on his feet.

This never happened. Jack never changed his lifestyle and continued to overspend. He always kept his income separate from Lisa's, and extended deeper into credit every month to fund his lifestyle.

He told his wife that when his parents passed away, his inheritance would eliminate their debt and provide them with the funds needed for retirement. He did not curb his spending, nor did he change his lifestyle. Lisa never really knew exactly how much they owed until their next life change. Jack had a fatal heart attack at age fifty-nine. He left his wife and two sons with a mountain of debt. His parents paid for the funeral.

THIRTY-SIX MONTHS LATER

Lisa was forced to sell everything to pay creditors, and moved into a one-bedroom condo close to the hospital where she worked. She had $75,000 left over from the life insurance proceeds to start a new life, with only a small mortgage of $120,000 on her new condo. Her boys were old enough to be out on their own, and both had jobs, trying to make a life for themselves.

COACH'S MESSAGE

Sometimes being downsized or let go from your employer can be a good thing, a blessing in disguise, perhaps allowing you to refocus on more important life events. It might even force you to change your career to pursue opportunities that you might not have thought possible in your old circumstances. I have seen many people prosper after being downsized and some who have said it pointed them in a different life direction that turned out to be more profitable. When life throws us a lemon, turn it around and make lemonade!

Lisa and Jack's situation was tragic and unfortunate. Many clients live far above their incomes, and count on a future inheritance to provide the much-needed retirement savings they had not been able to accumulate during their working years. We often see clients in their fifties and sixties who are only just starting to save for the future. Most find they are frustrated with how much debt they have, and have given up trying to reduce it, or they announce they are postponing their retirement plans and continuing to work.

Typically, men are more willing to accept risk with their finances. However, it is important for both partners to be involved in the financial decision process. I have found that the most financially successful couples were those that combined their incomes, working together to spend and save for their future. Those couples that kept their finances separate or secret with separate accounts and liabilities were always worse off. I have not seen one example in eighteen years of lending, where keeping separate money worked. One partner is always languishing, and the debts get higher while the savings never grow. It just doesn't work. Unlike Lisa and Jack, your finances have to be a team effort.

If you are married and plan to retire together, you must save and dissolve your debt together. There is strength in becoming unified together toward your own personal journey to wealth. Create a simple structure to increase your net worth, and begin a budgeted plan to eliminate your debt. If a new budget is not enough to trim the fat from your monthly expenses because of too much debt, downsizing your lifestyle might be another option. Have the strength to view your financial situation like a banker, not with the emotional need that got you into this position. The reality is, if you are living paycheque to paycheque and not making a dent in your debt or savings, something has to give. You must have the inner strength to deal with this situation now, during your earning years, when you can fix the problem. You don't want to be dealing with it in your sixties, when there is less time to recover. If you are counting on an inheritance, treat this as a windfall when you get it, rather than a band-aid. Having your finances in order will ensure that this new-found money can be used for other "dream" things, rather than just paying off debt that you have been continuously carrying with high interest year over year.

Do not forget to protect your family in the event of your death or disability. Most people know they need to be insured, but the average North American does not have enough insurance either because of the cost or because they think nothing will happen. Spend the time reviewing your insurance coverage and make sure you have the proper policies to protect yourself and your family. Speak to a professional, and always make sure you have a separate policy outside of your work plan. If you are laid off or change jobs, you need to ensure that you are still protected. Most new employers have probationary periods before coverage kicks in, and you do not want to be underinsured. Most plans are less expensive than people believe, translating into a couple of dollars a day. Usually, peace of mind can be obtained at a cost of a daily latte—something you can easily squeeze into your budget for asset protection.

By creating a joint budget that is tailored with both incomes and savings, you force yourselves to get accustomed to a new financial lifestyle, both making decisions and plans for the future. Your workable plan helps remove any uncertainties and creates unified stability to ensure together you become debt-free and comfortable at retirement.

RELYING ON HOME EQUITY TO FUND RETIREMENT: TRACIE AND KYLE

I hear it all the time from clients who say they are going to enjoy their life now and not worry about retirement; they might not even live long enough. Well, yes that is true, but most likely you will live a very long time, and then what?

This is usually a cry for help, when people feel like they have tried everything and can't improve their current financial situation. Telling yourself to live for the present to rationalize your spending will actually create more anxiety as time goes on about the uncertainties of tomorrow. Think how you will feel when you only have a few years left before you retire and have saved nothing. The reality is that, when you have your finances in order and are saving for the future, you feel better, you have less anxiety, and you feel more empowered and secure. This is why we buy so much life and disability insurance every year. We need the security to make sure our loved ones are looked after if we die. So, what about if you live—will you have enough?

I ran into Tracie one day when I was out shopping and we stopped to chat. Tracie was visibly stressed, and you could tell she was carrying a heavy burden of financial worry. She was turning fifty this year and her husband was fifty-one. They had no savings and mounting expenses now that both kids were in university. Tracie and Kyle were living paycheque to paycheque and supplementing their income with credit. The debt was growing, and the worry and uncertainty were poisoning Tracie's personality and outlook on life. Tracie and Kyle both believed they would have to rely on their home equity when they retired because they wouldn't have saved enough. They were unsure if they could pay off their mortgage, and thought they would probably have to sell their home to use the proceeds to fund their future. I convinced Tracie to have a financial plan done, and we agreed to meet again to look at options.

When you know you are going to be comfortable and secure at retirement, you feel better. Ask anyone who has no mortgage if they are worried about paying their bills. The anxiety and stress have been replaced with calm certainty. This is what Tracie and Kyle desperately needed, and this is exactly what they were able to achieve over time.

When we went over their debt and expenses, it was clear that they did not have enough income month to month. They would need to curb their spending and find ways to cut back, resisting the temptation to supplement their income with credit. With four refinances in the past to consolidate debt, their mortgage was now at $420,000 on a home worth $650,000. They had approximately $32,000 in credit card debt, and after reviewing Kyle's stock options at work, they had just over $105,000 in locked-in savings. Kyle's income was $132,000, a good income; however, he did not have a pension plan. Tracie made $21,500 running a home-based business. They had just booked a family holiday and planned to pay for it on credit, so we needed to add in another $15,000 in upcoming debt. Their net worth was $304,000.

SO WHAT DID THEY DO?

When you do not have enough money month to month and it seems as though there are demands from every direction, you need to stop the madness and take control. Constantly feeling helpless but unwilling to make the necessary changes only perpetuates the problem, and Tracie and Kyle had decided to do whatever it took. It would be fifteen years before they both reached sixty-five, and they were anxious to make the change. It was time to concentrate on managing their future, rather than living in the past with regrets and memories of broken plans.

It was necessary to create a separate savings plan in addition to paying off their mortgage. Paying off your mortgage and owning your home is considered to be one of the greatest financial accomplishments; however, you cannot rely completely on this investment to fund your future.

The solutions we planned to suggest would be life changing for this couple, and would involve a total re-evaluation of their current lifestyle and a concerted effort on their part. We wanted them to cut their discretionary spending drastically and live solely on Kyle's $132,000 income. We also wanted them to consider increasing their income to dissolve their debt and begin saving. There are lots of ways to make more money. You can get a promotion at your current job, perhaps start a consulting or freelance business part time, or maybe you need to retrain and go back to school. Whatever it is, this is a journey of self-discovery. I know it takes a lot of courage to get out of your comfort zone and challenge yourself for more than what you are right now, but it is worth it.

We asked this couple to answer the following questions: How much money do you have left over every month, and what are you willing to sacrifice from your lifestyle to lower expenses? What are you willing to give up and change?

Start to think about the big picture. Find out exactly what your current lifestyle costs. If you continue to do nothing, there eventually will be a consequence for your complacency. Be honest with your finances. Get a piece of paper and make a list of all your expenses and debts on one side of the page, and then on the other side list your income. Is there enough? Can you pay all your monthly expenses without turning to credit? Are there funds left over to save? If not, something has to change, and the only one to do it is you.

First we needed to ensure that we eliminated all of Tracie and Kyle's debt and set up a savings plan to provide income when they retired. Basically, we wanted to have approximately $100,000 in an nonregistered fund, such as a tax-free savings account (TFSA), and another $500,000 saved in an investment fund that could provide protection of capital and compounded long-term growth.

Using the Finance Tracker, we were able to cut monthly costs so that we could begin to live solely on Kyle's income. This was the key to their savings solution, and we believed this would create the necessary habits they would need when on a fixed income in retirement. We also reduced the amortization on their mortgage from eighteen to fifteen years, a minimal increase that was manageable. This new amortization would now match the amount of time until Tracie reached age sixty-five.

We also needed a plan to eliminate their $42,000 in credit card debt. Kyle took the initiative and started doing some consulting work on the side; this additional income could be used to pay off the credit faster. Still, we set up a scheduled payment plan with the aid of their Tracker to keep the commitments top of mind.

The education costs were the next hurdle that had to be addressed, but we had already made their budget extremely tight, with no additional funds for this expense. Tracie and Kyle had some hard choices to make, and decided to include their kids in their discussions. It turned out that their son wanted to switch to a co-op program that offered paid work experience, and he was very willing to pay for the rest of his two-year education. With his parents' help in co-signing, he could apply for a small student loan for the balance of his education that he could pay off easily and that would help him build good credit for the future. Tracie and Kyle wanted to keep things equal between their two children, so they agreed to pay for the next two years of education for their daughter, who was only in her first year of university. This would allow her to save for any additional education she might want, or perhaps she would opt to follow the same route as her brother. Either way, it was fair, and the kids and parents were happy with this compromise. So this meant we had to find two years' worth of education funds.

From where?

It was necessary for Tracie to go back into the workforce to increase her annual income. We not only needed her income to help with the upcoming education costs; we also needed to start our savings program. Through her home-based business contacts, Tracie was able to get a permanent job earning $58,000. This was great news, and even better was the fact that this job offered a pension plan and an employee stock option. With Tracie's added benefits at work, Kyle could now dial back on his family coverage for dental and prescription drugs so that his take-home pay would increase slightly. If Tracie decided to work for this employer until retirement, she could count on a pension income to supplement the government pension allowances for them both. We agreed to let the dust settle and allow Tracie and Kyle to adjust to their new lifestyle. We planned to meet again to look at investment options for their long-term future.

TWENTY-FOUR MONTHS LATER

When we met again, I was astounded by the difference in this newly empowered couple, especially Tracie. She had become more confident, happier, and focused. She was no longer withdrawn and miserable. Instead, she had this sureness about her and a spring in her voice. Both Kyle and Tracie had replaced uncertainty with a sense of purpose, and had a plan to fix and rise above their debt.

The credit card debt was gone, and still using their Trackers they were able to save $6,300 as a rainy-day fund. The educational costs were now gone, and Tracie and Kyle were excited to begin their plan for retirement. We now had only thirteen years to go. We knew they could live on Kyle's income quite comfortably with their son moved out and their daughter rarely at home. Kyle was still consulting on the side, and his little business had grown quite nicely. This was something he felt he could continue once retired to supplement their income. Tracie's income could be saved and used for retirement.

Kyle's consulting income would be saved into tax-free savings products, one for each of them. Here, we could invest the funds in blue chip and bank stocks to ensure an estimated $75,000 each at retirement in thirteen years. Tracie's net income of approximately $35,000 could be saved in an investment plan for both of them. We decided to use a fixed income portfolio of institutional compounding bonds. This would ensure the preservation of their capital, with a secure compounded growth. We could have entertained leverage lending or other investment products, but Tracie and Kyle were very conservative and wanted to keep their risk as low as possible. The $105,000 from Kyle's employer was also invested in the same manner.

Their projected net worth at retirement would be $1,598,000. We followed the investment strategy outlined in the chapter on Retirement Dreaming and used the Bucket Approach. This included $150,000 in their TFSA/honeymoon fund, $548,000 in their investment fund, and the projected value of their home at $900,000. Tracie would have a pension of $630 per month plus their government pension allowances. During the first five to seven years of retirement, they would live on Kyle's part-time income, and they could use their honeymoon fund, tax free, to travel and have fun. Their mortgage would be paid, and the annual costs of continuing to live in their home would be minimal. As a backup plan, if needed, they could downsize and invest the proceeds in the same manner. The investments, after an additional seven years, would be worth $762,000 from continuous compounded growth at 4.5%. Kyle's $105,000 was also invested in the same way, and could now be used as a long-term fund for old age care if needed. This fund would be worth $290,100.

Tracie and Kyle completely turned things around by increasing their net worth by $1,294,000 and eliminating their debt. They are to be commended for their learned monetary budgeting and their tremendous courage and tenacity to make changes in their careers and increase their income.

COACH'S MESSAGE

There is no reason for you not to retire wealthy unless you hold yourself back. These clients changed their focus and began concentrating on managing their future, rather than living in the past. It's okay to have your past experiences, but you don't want them to keep you from moving forward. You need to break through your fear of not having enough money at retirement and stop limiting yourself. By choosing to pay off their home along with building a retirement savings fund, Tracie and Kyle created a life full of options and possibilities. If you want to have a comfortable retirement, you need to invest the time and energy to get in the game and get on with it. Tracie and Kyle really made drastic changes to their budget and became great savers. The choice to go back into the workforce to a conventional job was a big decision for Tracie and one that she said she was glad she made.

Consider continually analyzing your net worth to monitor your ongoing saving success. It is viewed as your financial snapshot, measuring growing assets against personal debt. You will need to monitor your net worth regularly and ensure that it is increasing year over year. Due to the growing lack of savings, some people are planning to use their homes as the sole source of their retirement income. Considered by most to be their biggest financial asset, it is no surprise that most will not make the necessary sacrifices to save for the future, and may become jaded by inflated net worth statements based on the projected increased house values. Be careful. Relying solely on your equity could leave you with less than you think if the market severely declines.

Build a separate savings portfolio and resist the urge to use your home as your only retirement savings. Above all, make sure to pay off your debt. Statistics show a steady decline in personal savings since the early 1990s, and many people are still retiring with mortgage debt. Most believe they will sell their home and downsize. Ask yourself: "How much are you planning to spend on this smaller home?" or, "Are you going to have to move to an apartment to liquidate the funds you now need to live on in retirement?"

In surveys, more than half of all people about to enter retirement said they had changed their mind about selling their home, and 40% said they were not sure if they planned to do so in the near future. Don't be forced into selling your home in retirement because of your declining financial situation. Save during your working years and build a financial portfolio so that you can provide yourself with a strong foundation of security and choices in the future. Even though we are now enjoying a relatively stable housing market with increasing values, remember that if house prices decline, you don't want the worry of having to sell your home for less than you expected. Having the freedom to choose, because you don't need to sell your home, ensures you will not be forced into making sacrifices and choices that you might not want to make.

HOW CAN WE SAVE FOR RETIREMENT WHEN WE DON'T EARN ENOUGH? MANDY AND JOE

I was driving home one evening when I received a call from a familiar client. After chatting about family and current events, it was obvious that Mandy was upset about her current financial predicament. She was tired of living paycheque to paycheque and reaching for credit when she needed something extra for the kids. Saving for retirement is a wonderful notion if you have the extra funds to save every month. But what if you are stretched so thin you just can't afford to maintain your lifestyle? We have all heard the advice from investment advisors and bankers who tell us to save 10% of our income, and have it deducted at source so we get used to living on less. Okay—great idea if you can afford it. But what if you can't spare that 10% and need every penny you earn to keep food on the table and a roof over your head.

Mandy and Joe on paper looked okay, but in reality they were drowning. Joe earned $71,500 as a manager of a local credit union, and Mandy was a customer service representative earning $28,000. They had two teenage boys who would need financial assistance if they planned to further their education, but since Mandy and Joe had not been able to save over the years, there was nothing available to help them out. With no savings and mounting debt, Mandy was desperate for a solution. She felt the only way to help her boys and get rid of their current debt was to do what she had always done: refinance her mortgage to the maximum the banks would allow. Their home was worth $350,000 and they had a mortgage of $223,500. They had credit card debt totalling approximately $24,000 and a line of credit maxed at $13,500. Mandy was fifty-three and Joe was forty-nine. Both could expect a small pension from their employer when they retired, but felt they could not afford to contribute to these plans from their already-stretched monthly income. Their net worth was $89,000.

Joe always felt he could keep working, and had another sixteen years before he reached sixty-five. He believed they had plenty of time to pay off their debt and save for the future. Always putting off saving can become a habit that is easily justified with daily living expenses and must-haves for the kids and home. Life is expensive, and even though your income might go up over time, it sometimes seems that there is never quite enough to get ahead and save for the future. I have seen this with many clients who reach retirement with outstanding debt and little to no savings, declaring that they just don't know how it happened. You must start actively participating in your financial future. Before you know it, you will be only a few years from retirement, and you might find yourself in the same situation with no more time to recover.

Unless you make a plan and take action toward your financial security, you might find yourself wondering what to do at the end of your working years. We all want to have an enriched, comfortable retirement lifestyle, where you can enjoy doing the things you want to do, rather than just filling your days with mundane tasks to fill up time.

I met with Mandy and Joe, and although I knew they wanted to refinance again, I wanted to offer them a better solution—one we could use to build a retirement future on and increase their net worth.

SO WHAT DID THEY DO?

First, it was important to instil in Mandy and Joe the courage to realize it was time to create a plan and make the necessary changes to fix their finances. We needed them to stop the "band-aid" approach of continuously refinancing debt and to realize that they were so much more than their current financial situation. By making the right changes, they absolutely could set themselves up for future success. It was time for these clients to take back control and get off the rollercoaster ride of living paycheque to paycheque.

The immediate need was to eliminate debt and reduce unnecessary high-interest charges. The other priority was to set up an education fund for the boys, so that they would have financial assistance for any trade school, college, or university that they wanted to pursue. Mandy and Joe had also wanted to upgrade their home, which they had purchased fifteen years ago and refinanced every couple of years to consolidate debt. New homes usually have the greatest increase in value during the first ten years, then level off to nominal market increases. Joe felt they needed to put on a new roof in the next five years and consider upgrading the kitchen and bathrooms.

When we chatted about their long-term plans, they said they both had always wanted to retire back in the small town where Mandy grew up. There, house prices were much less and the slower pace of small-town living was perfect for their retirement plans. They mentioned that they would love to travel every year if they could afford it, but thought this would probably not be a reality, since they believed they might never have enough disposable income in their later years.

To put together a completely customized plan, you must go deeper with your hopes, dreams, and aspirations. You must look at all facets of your current situation, and try to determine logically where you plan to be in the future. If you have older teenage children, involve them in this plan and see what thoughts they have for their own futures. Be truthful with yourself. Once you have a clear, concise plan of improvement, you will feel empowered and will know where you are going. We asked these clients to write down what they wanted over the next year, the next five years, and the next ten. With these future plans in mind, we were able to develop a customized strategy for success. All that was then needed was for Mandy and Joe to make it happen!

When reviewing the solution, we contacted the client's current bank to get the best lending rate offer. If we were to consolidate the line of credit ($13,500) and the credit card debt ($24,000) along with the mortgage ($223,500) and the estimated home improvements ($30,000), the new mortgage would be $291,000. The bank advised us it would blend their current mortgage rate and could offer 4.9% on a new mortgage. This would put their monthly payment at $1,675 if the loan was amortized over twenty-five years. But we did not have twenty-five years until retirement!

This is the option that all bankers suggest, and it is good business for the lending institution but not the best option for the client. You need to think outside the "banking box" and create opportunities for yourself. We suggested that instead of refinancing and upgrading their home, they sell it. Yes, sell it! When we discussed their work environment with the clients, we learned that Joe took the train to work and drove his car to the station, where it sat all day in the elements. Why not consider moving closer to work and downsizing your home to something new and modern, with the potential for increased equity growth over the next few years? By buying a home that is under a year old, you can take advantage of the market growth over the next ten years and give your net worth an instant lift.

At first, this was a very difficult consideration to accept and very much out of their comfort zone. We suggested that, if they sold their home, they would be able to use the proceeds to pay off their credit cards and line of credit and, more important, get out of their high-interest mortgage with their current lender. If they could sell their home for $355,000, we would even be able to set up an education fund for their boys.

With the prospects of eliminating their debt and having an education fund for the kids, Mandy and Joe began looking around for a new home, and decided to find out how they would go about selling their current home. We also suggested they start tracking their spending using the Finance Tracker and a daily Cash Journal so that we could determine how to rein in spending and begin saving for retirement. If we reduced the large costs of housing and car expenses, we could free up cash every month to begin living on a more comfortable budget without reaching for credit to supplement necessities.

12 MONTHS LATER

Mandy and Joe found a beautiful three-bedroom executive townhouse within walking distance of Joe's commuter train for work. They sold their home through a realtor for $361,000, and were able to get a deal on the realtor's commission by purchasing the townhouse through the same representative. With the sale proceeds, Mandy and Joe were able to pay off all their outstanding debt, with $28,000 left over after their down payment on their new home. The $28,000 was split in half and put into a managed high-interest education fund for each of their boys to use when they were ready. Their younger son had to adjust to a change of high schools now that they had moved to another area. Their eldest son was in his last year of high school and was planning to go to a trade school in the city, soon to be taking the commuter train in the mornings like his father. There was a bit of resistance about the move from their kids, and Mandy was very concerned that they might not like it. Joe, on the other hand, thought it would be good for them to experience a change to better prepare them for adult life.

The education fund for each of the boys was small, only about $15,000, but Mandy and Joe had always let their boys know they would have to pay part of their education, and felt the boys would work harder if they had a vested interest in their own future by having to do so.

The townhouse was purchased for $290,000, with $58,000 down from the sale of their old home. Now they had a new mortgage of $232,000, which we placed with a different lender at a very competitive rate of 3%, amortized over sixteen years, matching the time left until Joe expected to finish working. The monthly payment of $1,460 was lower than they were used to, and with no other debts they found themselves living well within their means. Mandy was excited to see that there was extra money left over at the end of each month, and for the first time felt as though she was ahead of the game.

When we went over their daily Cash Journal and Finance Tracker for the previous six months, I did not have to make any recommendations, since Mandy was well on her way to doing this on her own. By simply keeping track of the money coming in and going out, you instantly start to realize how to cut back on frivolous spending and become a more aware and educated consumer. Now that we had the daily budget set up and the household and car expenses reduced, it was time to allocate funds toward savings. Both Mandy and Joe started contributing to their company pension plan and began putting away an additional $300 a month into an investment savings plan. We set up the savings plan as an automatic payment to come out monthly from their bank account. This forced saving was easily worked into their new budget, and could now grow to provide the travel fund that Mandy and Joe wanted when they retired.

We suggested that it would be necessary for them to increase their savings over time, and after discussions they planned to do so when the boys moved out. Mandy had decided to get a part-time job selling cosmetics through a home-party business. She had run a small, home-based business years ago and was looking for ways to increase her income. She was now making about $500 extra every month, and estimated she could add an additional $250 a month toward their savings plan, increasing it to $550 every month. This would give them approximately $118,000 at retirement if invested in a managed fund at 5%.

They had two vehicles, and with Joe's easy proximity to public transit, he decided to sell his car and was happy to have the reduced insurance and fuel costs. When they asked me what they should do with these funds, they were surprised by my answer. I suggested they use the money to go on a family vacation. Yes, it is a good idea to save and watch every penny, but you also have to enjoy your journey to retirement and not deprive yourself every day until you get there. Mandy and Joe had made some very tough decisions and had really changed their financial lives, setting themselves up for future success. They had not been on a family vacation for years, and now that the kids were older they would probably really enjoy it and would never forget it. Joe had wanted to take his boys back to Italy, and had not seen his mother for over twelve years. What a wonderful feeling it would be to go on a family trip completely paid for and not have to reach for credit or have a bill waiting for them when they returned.

At retirement, if Joe and Mandy continued with their current setup, they could expect to be debt-free with a projected net worth of $783,000, not including their monthly employee and government pension plans. We advised them to continue living on their current budget and to add any increases in income to their savings plan or put in an emergency fund for home improvement or for a new vehicle in the future. This would mean that they would be very used to living on a fixed budget when they start retirement and could look forward to more disposable income when the kids moved out. Through our discussions, if they were to save their estimated increased earnings, they could expect their net worth to be $896,000.

With over sixteen years to go, they could also entertain the idea of flipping real estate again. It is sometimes wise to consider selling your home once it has reached its peak value and purchasing new again in a lateral move to lower your mortgage even further. Newly built properties generally increase in value the greatest during the first five years, and could offer a welcome boost in equity that could lower your mortgage and get you to retirement faster. At retirement, if Joe and Mandy decided to move back to Mandy's small home town, they could then expect to purchase a home for much less, further ensuring they stay mortgage free. With their investment portfolio, work pensions, government pensions, and Old Age Security, this couple would have no future financial worries and could look forward to a long and comfortable retirement together.

COACH'S MESSAGE

Most of us, regardless of need, want to become wealthier. There is great comfort in knowing that there is money in the bank in case of an emergency. The lack of long-term resources for future retirement and current high debt loads can paralyze clients in their forties and fifties. It becomes a slow-burning anxiety that continues to grow into an all-out fire of fear as the years creep closer and closer to retirement. Bottom line: you must live within your means to save more and spend less. That's it.

Creating a budget to monitor daily and monthly cash flow is an excellent step for finding ways to trim your lifestyle. Sometimes all it takes is some simple changes to be less wasteful with our expenses. Taking your lunch to work, resisting impulse purchases, and cutting out memberships and extravagant trips can free up funds that can be saved or used to pay down debt. Mandy and Joe became great financial role models to their children. It is important to teach our kids to make compromises and to be okay if they don't get everything they want.

If you are not making enough money every month and have to go to credit to subsidize your lifestyle, then you must make a change. There are only two options. Downsize your expenses or earn more income.

Mandy and Joe did both. They downsized their overall expenses, tracked their spending, and looked for ways to increase their income. Remember, your greatest source of more money is your earning potential. Mandy decided to work part time in something she loved, but you can also look for ways to increase your income by taking advantage of opportunities with your current employer. Consider reading about successful people and become inspired. Just like your Finance Tracker, try an Encouragement Tracker. Keep a personal diary filled with uplifting and motivational thoughts just for you.

Most of all, believe that your life can only get better if you get better. You cannot defer happiness until you are retired. Be happy now with your family and realize that life provides endless opportunities for personal growth that will take you to new experiences and exciting new ventures. Go on a family holiday or take a mini-break to recharge, relax, and have fun. Enjoy the journey to reaching retirement. It is a treasure.

THE SANDWICH GENERATION: JENNIFER AND DAVE

A Canadian couple, Jennifer and Dave, both fifty-six, were perfect examples of the "sandwich generation" phenomenon. They had two girls in university and were supplementing Dave's parents, who were now retired. The added strain of helping elderly parents is a new, possibly continuing dilemma for some aging clients entering retirement with insufficient portfolios. For those with kids, providing financial assistance seems inevitable, since the average age of children leaving home is now twenty-seven.

Many clients now feel they are sandwiched between the commitment to help their children and the added strain of assisting elderly parents. Nowadays, many aging parents have little or no inheritance for their children, which has increased the pressure on aging clients to come up with their own financial funding for their future. With the complications of financially assisting parents and the added pressures of children now staying at home longer than they did twenty years ago, saving for retirement can seem like a pipe dream.

The burden of two necessary expenditures was taking its toll on this couple. Dave's dad was on disability and his mom had a small pension, but due to low savings and poor investment decisions, they had very little to live on. They were forced into retirement earlier than anticipated, and never dreamed they would now need the allowance that their only son provided every month. Dave was unhappy with his parents' predicament, and wanted them to sell their home, pay off their mortgage, and move into an affordable apartment. They were reluctant to do this, but knew something had to change.

Both Jennifer and Dave had a secure income and together had investments totalling $420,000. Their home was worth $600,000 and they had a mortgage of $190,000. Paying down their mortgage and continuing to invest were very important to them; however, they just couldn't find a way to save any extra funds, month to month. Their net worth was $830,000. Their goal was to increase their investment portfolio to at least $500,000, and they wanted to have their home paid off. With the added expenditures, they didn't see how this target could be met. Cutting out the assistance to Dave's parents was not an option, so he planned to continue working after he was sixty-five.

Many people approaching retirement, like Jennifer and Dave, might not see retirement as a hard stop to working. By easing into retirement, you can postpone withdrawals from savings, therefore allowing your money to continue to grow and ultimately last longer. This should not cause you to put the brakes on future saving because of your anticipated continued work scenario, even if it is a planned part-time arrangement. If you are forced to retire earlier, you must ensure there is enough money to live on and continue to grow in a good savings program. Remember that life happens while you are making other plans. Don't get caught with less because you kept putting it off, assuming you had more time.

SO WHAT DID THEY DO?

The number one need of older clients is security, and this is what Dave wanted for himself and for his parents. Before we got started, it was necessary to discuss their budget and how they were coping with their expenditures. Jennifer and Dave were quite comfortable with the current monthly arrangements, but said they could not afford to contribute any more toward a saving plan. Currently, they were paying $800 a month for the girls' education, $1,000 to Dave's parents, and $2,510 to their mortgage. With very little left over for food, taxes, utilities, and entertainment, they made it very clear they could not stretch their already-tight monthly budget.

The solution I presented to this couple not only would allow them to stay within their prescribed monthly budget; it would also provide them a tax-free savings plan for their future. The first thing I wanted them to consider was changing the amortization on their current mortgage from seven years to nine years—we could pull back the amortization to match the years left when Jennifer and Dave reached sixty-five. This would make the monthly payment a little smaller, and would allow us room for the next part of our solution. It was evident that Dave's parents needed to change their predicament, and we would need buy-in from all parties to proceed with the next steps in this process. Here is what we suggested.

We suggested that Dave's parents sell their home, use the proceeds of the sale to pay off their debt, and invest the balance, together with their other savings, into an annuity that would provide a fixed income for the next twenty years. Dave's parents were seventy-six and seventy-eight years old. The annuity plus their pension would give them a comfortable lifestyle once their debt was eliminated. Close to Jennifer and Dave was a new condominium development that was offering units from $150,000. We recommended Dave's parents purchase a small new condo so that they could continue to enjoy home ownership. But we wanted Dave to provide the down payment and be the guarantor to the mortgage. This would mean the parents could keep their annuity intact and continuing to grow.

Alone, Dave's parents could not afford to purchase this property, but by having their son assist them, they could enjoy a new home while he gained an appreciating asset. Simply purchasing the condo in Dave's name and then letting his parents live in it would not have provided Dave any benefit. He could not have used the property as a tax write-off since his parents would not have been paying rent, and the government disallows family members as legitimate "arm's-length" tenants.

Together with his parents, Dave found a ground-floor condo for $210,000. Here is how we set up their new plan.

The 20% down payment needed for the purchase would be $42,000, which we added to Dave's current mortgage on his home. By adjusting the amortization to nine years, the time remaining until Jennifer and Dave both reached sixty-five, the payment was actually $50 lower than their existing budgeted monthly payment at a seven-year amortization.

Existing Plan:

- Current mortgage = $190,000
- Mortgage payment at seven years' amortization = $2,508
- Budgeted allowance to parents = $1,000
- Budgeted school costs to kids = $800

Total monthly costs = $4,308

New Plan:
- New mortgage on home = $232,000 ($190,000 + $42,000 down payment on condo)
- Mortgage payment at nine years' amortization = $2,451*
- Budgeted allowance to parents = $1,050**
- Budgeted school costs to kids = $800

Total monthly costs = $4,301

* *$57 less per month.*
** *Dave's parents took a new $168,000 mortgage, amortized over seventeen years, with Dave as the guarantor. This monthly payment would be $1,050, only $50 higher than the allowance Dave had committed to continue paying his parents.*

Essentially, Dave continued with his current monthly expenditures, but allowed his parents to move into a new, modern, more suitable home, with no debt burden and an annuity that provided a comfortable lifestyle. We changed Dave's parents' Will to give him Power of Attorney and to ensure that the property would pass to Jennifer and Dave upon their death. Because it was the parents' primary residence, it would be exempted from taxes, and therefore Dave could realize the increased value without capital gains tax. We estimated that the property would double in value in ten years, since it was purchased new, but it actually took only eight years to do so. We also ensured that Dave increased his whole life insurance policy by $210,000, which would eliminate the additional debt in the event of his premature death. An added bonus was that, with this increase to their insurance policy, Jennifer and Dave could choose to use the additional funds in their cash surrender value when they retired.

To ensure that Jennifer and Dave's investments continued to grow with minimal capital depreciation, we chose a laddered investment portfolio for their $420,000 RSP portfolio. A collection of institutional compounding investments at 5.5% provided a return of $680,232 at retirement. Jennifer and Dave's net worth at age sixty-five was $1,865,000, more than double what they started with nine years ago. Their home was valued at $750,000 and was free and clear. The mortgage, which included the 20% down payment on Dave's parents' condo purchase, had been paid off. The condo was valued at $430,000 and had a mortgage balance of $88,648. Jennifer and Dave's investment portfolio was valued at just over $692,000, and they also had $41,300 available if needed in their whole life policies.

We didn't make any monetary changes to their monthly budget, but rather acquired an appreciating asset and changed the dynamics of an existing situation for a better solution for all. The parents, kids, Jennifer, and Dave were all happy and living well. Jennifer retired and spent time with her in-laws almost every day, while Dave continued to work at a slower pace, now only fifteen hours per week.

COACH'S MESSAGE

Financially assisting our children is inevitable, and most parents are feeling the pinch. Adding in the expense of elderly parents usually creates a tremendous strain not uncommon for today's clients. Indeed, almost 60% of couples over age fifty provide some kind of care and monetary assistance to grown children and aging parents. A continuing demographic shift faces aging clients that could reduce or eliminate any hopes of an inheritance for future generations. Couple this with the increased volatility of the markets and rising inflation, and it is easy to see why more investment advisors are predicting the shrinkage of future inheritances for the millennial generation. Accordingly, you should establish a good customized financial solution and personalized strategy to protect your future and maximize the transfer of wealth.

In this solution, Jennifer and Dave decided to forgo joint ownership of the condominium with Dave's parents. Joint ownership allows other owners on title through joint tenancy with the right of survivorship. All owners would have full access to the property, and if one owner dies, the property passes to the surviving owners and bypasses the estate. This is a good option, but we did not want joint ownership in Jennifer and Dave's case. The transfer of property on death passes to the surviving spouse without taxation, but if the joint owner is not the spouse, it is considered a deemed disposition or sale at market value, and is subject to taxes upon the death of one owner. So, be careful when considering a joint ownership arrangement, and always consult your accountant. The death of a joint owner who is not your spouse will cause a dissolution on your personal share, and it is mandatory for all joint owners to declare annually their portion of income or capital gains to the Canada Revenue Agency (CRA).

By having every detail properly laid out in a will, we were able to ensure that the wishes of all parties were clearly defined and the property would be inherited without capital gains tax, since it was the parents' primary residence. If Dave were to die before his parents, the property would pass only to the surviving grandchildren, Jennifer and Dave's girls. From the beginning, Dave was always committed to helping his parents, but was unhappy about being forced to cut back on his savings plans for his own retirement. Without increasing the monthly budget, we were able to create a future appreciating asset that he would inherit virtually tax free, proving to be an even better investment than a rental property or registered savings plan.

Always make sure that you discuss your plans with your professional team—accountant, lawyer, advisor—so that they can provide up-to-date tax and legal advice. Do not underestimate the value of insurance when you are planning this strategy, so that you will always be protected against any unexpected negative circumstances.

WE CAN NEVER SAVE ENOUGH:
WENDY AND RAYMOND

On occasion I come across clients who have done everything right over the years and have become very wealthy just by doing it their way. This is the story of a good friend of mine whom I have known for over twenty-five years. Although Wendy's way of building wealth was kind of unorthodox, nonetheless it worked beautifully. Wendy and Ray literally started with a very small savings balance by today's standards, but at the time it represented their life savings. Most people struggle, save what they can, and believe they will never be able to amass true wealth because they just don't earn enough. Some even avoid getting into the housing market, believing they could not possibly handle all the extra costs of home ownership. This is a mistake. Over the past thirty years we have witnessed a continuous increase in home values, and by continuing to wait you may essentially buy yourself right out of the market. You must get in so that you can have this asset grow and provide you with the security for your latter years. But how will you make your payments once you buy? How can you pay down your debt and become mortgage free if you really can afford only to pay rent? While we agree that house prices have gone up considerably, it has never been a better time to buy into the market. Today's first-time homebuyers can purchase a home with only 5% down, and will enjoy interest rates that have not been this low since the 1940s. Here is the story of how one young couple took $42,000 and turned it into a net worth of over $1,290,000.

Let's start at the beginning. I first met Wendy at a bank I was affiliated with years ago where she worked as a full-time teller. We instantly became good friends, and I would meet her for coffee from time to time. Wendy and Ray had been married for about seven years and rented an apartment in the city. They had only one car and were voracious savers. Wendy was an avid coupon clipper, and could run circles around anyone who might think they could find a better deal than her. She never bought anything new, and even her clothes came from a thrift store. I was really surprised when I found this out, because frankly she always looked good. This was my first real epiphany about finding other ways to save money. Actually, at the time, I was quite in awe of how she could stretch a dollar.

People rarely, myself included, go to the extremes that Wendy did. Most would feel deprived, cheated, or miserable if they had to do without, as Wendy and Ray did. But they were not unhappy; in fact, they were among my nicest and most enjoyable clients to be around. Ray worked for the oil and gas industry as a tank inspector and made $51,000. Wendy earned $17,500 as a central teller for a national bank. I often encouraged Wendy and Ray to consider buying a home, rather than renting, and use their savings as the down payment. At the time, you had to put down 25%, and they could have purchased a home for $150,000. Wendy was always unsure about giving up her savings, but I knew she really wanted to own a home and maybe have children. Eventually we met to discuss her plan. She had talked it over with her parents, and had decided to purchase a home, as they had done. I was confused at first, but as the story unravelled it became crystal clear.

Wendy was the youngest of five girls, and her mother stayed at home. Her dad never earned much as a custodian at a local recreation centre, so her parents had to be very frugal. Their backyard was converted into a giant vegetable garden, and all the girls took part canning, pickling, and preserving everything. Three girls shared the largest bedroom, Wendy and her sister shared another, and her parents had the smallest bedroom, which they apparently still use today, even though all the girls are married and have moved out. They live in a three-storey walk-up in the city, and for increased revenue Wendy's dad had part-time jobs and her parents always had boarders in the basement and upstairs.

Wendy and Ray wanted to buy a home next to the university, and planned to have boarders to help pay down the mortgage. I must say this took me back a little—I had visions of Wendy and Ray packing their new home full of students and charging rent for every room. The banks back then (and especially now) did not like to lend money for homes used for nonconforming rentals or rooming houses. Properties need to have the correct zoning as either a duplex or triplex, with specific standards met for fire code regulations. I was a little nervous, and advised them of our concerns.

While I am the first one to say that the fastest way to increase your capital is through your potential to earn more income, I wasn't sure how well this plan would work. However, one should never underestimate the creativity and commitment of someone who wants to better their circumstances. Wendy did not want to have boarders intermingling with their living space, but planned to find a home that could accommodate tenants upstairs and downstairs. Ray planned to make the upgrades himself, modifying their new home to accommodate tenant living spaces, equipping them with small kitchenettes, separate bathrooms, and, of course, a separate entrance. Wendy worked tirelessly with the city to ensure they met the residential guidelines, and even had a city inspector come out before they finalized their purchase.

They settled on a 1920s three-storey home four blocks from the university for $147,500. It was in desperate need of repair and updating, but Wendy and Ray were thrilled with their purchase. Their down payment was $37,000, and they began a new mortgage of $110,500 at a rate of 9.241%. They were finally homeowners. Ray's parents were also happy about their purchase and gave them $8,000. It turned out that Ray's brother had borrowed money from their parents to buy his first home and never paid it back, so his parents gave Ray the same amount to keep it fair. This was a welcome injection to their already-tight budget, and they planned to use these funds together with another $4,000 to upgrade their home. Now, I know what you are thinking here: $12,000 is not a lot of money. But this was also twenty-four years ago. Wendy made this money go as far as it could. She went to junkyards, liquidation centres, and even a place called "Mr. Used" to purchase all the things they needed to upgrade their home for student tenants. Then she advertised around the campus, and in no time she had two renters upstairs and three renters downstairs.

Her student rentals were clean and quaint, each room having an Old World charm to it because of the age of their home. Wendy interviewed and carefully screened all the would-be tenants to ensure she had good students who wanted a quiet place to call home. All her tenants were second- and third-year students who were used to living in crowded dorm rooms with noisy roommates. Over time, Wendy had a great little business that allowed her to stay at home when she had her first child. She always looked after her boarders, and I was surprised to hear that she would bake them cookies, do their laundry on occasion, and even pick up things for them at the store. There was a noise curfew of 10:00 P.M., but this changed to 7:00 P.M. when her son was little. Her students didn't seem to mind. She was quick to evict any bad tenants within the three-month probation period on her lease agreements. She was never without a boarder. It seems that word had gotten around campus, and Wendy had a waiting list for every semester.

After a while, Wendy had permanent tenants who wanted to stay. She had a history professor who taught at the university and a young science student who stayed for many years while he went to medical school and then got his PhD. When they moved to a larger home on the same street, Wendy and Ray made sure the purchase could accommodate their permanent boarders. They had lived in their previous home for seven years, and had paid down the mortgage to $11,700. They sold for $290,000, and purchased their new home for $501,000. They only needed approximately $235,000; however, they added $40,000 to this amount for upgrades and modifications to the property. Their new mortgage for this purchase was $275,000.

As before, they customized their home to accommodate student tenants, and began using the extra income to pay down their mortgage. Wendy went back to work full time when their son began school at an income of $23,700. Ray's income with the same employer was now $68,400. They both always contributed to their employee pension programs and had good dental and health coverage from their employers. It was now they also began contributing to their company's savings plan, which their employer matched up to 6%. It is a good idea to investigate your own savings programs with your employer, since most large companies have some form of assisted retirement savings plan.

After about ten years, their mortgage was down to $18,000. This is a great example of how making lump sums to your mortgage debt can really make a difference. Let's look at how Wendy and Ray got their debt down.

Original mortgage amount:	**$275,000**
Amortized over 25 years = $1,461/month	
Balance after 10 years at 4.10%:	**$196,709**
Every year Wendy put down a lump sum:	**$14,200**
Tenant income and extra savings	
Mortgage balance after 10 lump sum payments:	**$18,590**

Like a small company hiring more employees to make their business more profitable, Wendy and Ray essentially had other people help them pay down their debt. "Mortgage helpers" is what Wendy called them.

This would be their last move. Wendy and Ray purchased their current home only one block from the university on a street they had always wanted to live on. It is a beautiful boulevard with century-old homes and mature trees that offer a breathtaking canopy of leaves in the summer and fall. The house was converted to a triplex, and would accommodate the three permanent tenants who followed them. Wendy and Ray purchased this home for $1.050.000 and sold their previous one for $890,000. They needed to qualify for a new mortgage of only $239,000, which they felt confident they could pay off by retirement. Ray's income was now $102,000, and Wendy was now making $48,300 as a customer service manager in a different division of the bank. Their son was now going to the nearby university, and enjoyed a very short walk to his classes. Today Wendy and Ray have approximately $95,000 each in their employee shared savings plans, they still own only one car, and their home is worth approximately $1,200,000. Their mortgage is now down to $98,000 and their net worth is $1,292,000. They both will continue working for another twelve years, and can expect to retire debt-free, each with good pensions and an above-average savings portfolio.

COACH'S MESSAGE

The idea of having boarders in your home is not new—it was common practice in the early 1900s. Today, however, most people would not want to take in a boarder, instantly giving up their personal space and privacy. That being said, this activity, now referred to as a homestay business, has become surprisingly popular with international students. The internet has opened up a whole new world of business opportunities, with some big companies now offering services to connect students and travellers with hosting families that are all part of a new network of temporary lodging facilities. I have heard they even now provide satisfaction ratings and star rankings for their host family participants.

If you are thinking of starting a small homestay business, make sure you have researched all the facts before you open up your home. Remember, you can never step away from it, and you will always have to be monitoring your tenants and interviewing potential new ones. Wendy and Ray never indulged in vacations away from home, something that most people today would not want to sacrifice.

This is a true home-based business, and, as such, must be reported on your tax return. Wendy and Ray always had their personal taxes done by an accountant who ensured they declared their rental income and took advantage of the many expenses they can write off every year. They always had comprehensive home insurance to protect themselves and their boarders, and kept up to date on the tenant rules and regulations. When they sold their home, they had to pay capital gains tax on a percentage of their home, and this was always declared properly with the CRA. Wendy became a very savvy businesswoman, and was always very upfront and honest. She screened her new boarders diligently, asking them to fill out a detailed application, requesting photo identification, references, and proof of income. She also obtained a credit report and a criminal check on all her chosen candidates. She would interview her new out-of-town students with their parents, and always requested a security/cleaning deposit upfront. This would be returned when the boarder moved out as long as the room was left in good condition. Wendy always had a list of house rules, and did not allow any pets or smoking in her home. She also had separate bank accounts for her business, and was a meticulous record keeper. You might think that Wendy was too regimented with her rules and choice of boarders, but her tenants loved her and would stay with her for years. She always had a waiting list for rooms, and often could not keep up with the demand. She really cared about her students and looked after them, something that parents really appreciated. Wendy became good friends with most of her boarders, and gladly provided character, academic, and job references.

You might wonder why Wendy and Ray upgraded their home once their mortgage was almost paid. Besides the obvious desire for a larger residence and perhaps acquiring more boarders, this was a great way to continue using qualified home expenses as future tax write-offs to lower their business income. Mortgage interest, property taxes, home insurance, and all utility expenses are legitimate write-offs to lower their income. Once the mortgage was paid, they lost this expenditure, and therefore considered upsizing to another home to take advantage of these write-offs again. They always kept their new mortgage at a conservative balance, choosing never to overextend themselves. They always wanted an amount they could easily pay off, and never used their business income to qualify for more. The secret to their success was that they lived within their means, and used all of their business income to pay down debt. This is a great way to increase net worth.

If you are thinking of having a boarder in your home, please discuss this with your accountant, and never think that you cannot declare this income on your tax return. All it takes is an anonymous tip to the CRA from a disgruntled neighbour or tenant, and you will be audited. Run your homestay business the right way. Do your homework and make a business plan. Consider your home location and whether you want to provide rooms for travellers, international students, or just people from your community. Will you cater to singles, business professionals, or have an age or income requirement? Whatever you choose, if you decide to entertain the homestay business and use, as Wendy calls them, "mortgage helpers," you could stand to make a lot of money, and will most likely reach your goals in half the time.

Good luck!

THE KIDS DESERVE IT ALL: ANNE AND ROBERT

Do our kids today really deserve more than we had growing up?

Most parents definitely feel they do. More than half of parents today believe they should provide more opportunities and more choices for their children. There are more private schools, more clubs, and more extracurricular activities for our young than ever before. We have become obsessed with providing an easier, more affluent lifestyle for our children. Some believe it is because parents today were not given the same opportunities, and therefore are overindulging their kids to make up for the things they wish they'd had. Now, I am not saying this is bad—on the contrary, it is great to have parents who are keen to become involved with the development and well-being of their children. It is believed that this new generation will be more nurturing parents and will be more educated and more socially and technologically prepared for adulthood than any generation before them.

But this is a book on money, not child psychology. Think again: you are spending too much money on your kids at the expense of your own savings and debt reduction. There must be a balance. Remember that love isn't measured by the dollars you spend.

Anne and Rob have one son, in competitive hockey, and two daughters, in competitive dance. They travelled around every week for their kids' events, and it had become a huge part of their family lifestyle. All three kids had gone to private school since kindergarten. The two girls were still in a private elementary school, in Grades 7 and 8, while the eldest, their son, was at a private high school, in Grade 11. Anne is a good friend of mine I have known for years. However, our relationship has never moved into a client-banker partnership. I really did not know how dire Anne and Rob's situation was until they came to me for financial advice.

On the surface, the couple portrayed an image of affluence. They dressed in designer clothes, drove expensive cars, were sending three kids to private school, and went on ski vacations every March Break. They lived in a large home in an affluent area, and for anyone looking at their life they had it all. This is quite typical. I see it often with many middle-class couples, and wonder when people will stop the spending madness. Anne was a sales representative for a high-tech digital solution company, and made $92,000 per year. Rob had a home renovation business that had decreasing sales in the previous five years because of a work-related injury. He had decided to go back to being a full-time electrician and was sure that his income would increase with new contracting jobs. Based on a three-year average, Rob's income was about $45,000 per year. Their home was now worth $850,000, with a mortgage of $751,800. They had $43,000 owing on credit cards, $32,000 on a line of credit, and an overdraft that never seemed to break free from its $5,000 monthly limit. They wanted to consolidate their debt into their mortgage, as they had done before, and believed if they could refinance up to 95% they could lower their interest charges. If possible, this would not eliminate all the outstanding debt, but it would help make their monthly payments easier.

I wondered how they were able to pay the private school tuition for all three children, which was more than Anne's annual net income. Apparently, Anne's parents helped out with these payments, and Anne confessed she owed her parents over $230,000, which she knew she could never repay. When we switched the conversation to savings and investments, there was little to get excited about. Together they had just under $73,000 saved and another $21,000 in a TFSA to help pay for the next school year. When I suggested cutting back on the kids' extracurricular activities and perhaps putting them in the public school system, this was flatly rejected by both.

The fact is, the banking system had changed drastically since Anne and Rob had done their last refinance. Over the years since the 2008 financial crisis, we have observed increasingly tightened lending practices. What we were able to do, even a year ago, would not be the same as what the banks would consider this year. Every year the banks are becoming more and more conservative, and seem to be almost "cherry-picking" better clients to lower potential future lending risks.

The 95% mortgage refinance was out of the picture. This was stopped years ago, and now homeowners can refinance with the banks only in a conventional manner—meaning only up to 80% of the house value. It is also important to note that this would be based on the bank's appraised value of the home, not the market value, which is always considerably higher. More clients today are getting a rude awakening to the new restrictions imposed by the banks. It is not the same lending landscape as it was years ago.

Anne was forty-seven and Robert forty-nine, both young enough to turn it around if they made some drastic changes. Unfortunately, those changes were not something this couple was willing to come to terms with yet. If Anne worked until sixty-five, she would have eighteen years to better their finances—definitely enough time to pay down the debt and start a retirement savings plan. Her employer did have a pension plan, to which she was not contributing. Anne could expect a small pension at retirement that she could use with government security as a good base for daily retirement living expenses. As for Rob, he should be maximizing his savings into investments every year to make up for his loss of pension security, since he was self-employed.

SO WHAT DID THEY DO?

Nothing. They were not ready to make the changes necessary to pay down debt and live within their income. For now, these clients would try to keep it going as long as they could, relying on Anne's parents to help them through when it really got tough. This was a financial house of cards ready to fall at the drop of any personal setback. What if Rob's business continued to decrease in revenue? What if Anne lost her job? Or worse, what if one of them got sick and couldn't work? Their relationship was strained by the financial pressure, but they were unwilling to correct their spending habits.

TWENTY-FOUR MONTHS LATER

Anne and Robert had separated, and the three kids were living with Anne and her parents. Their son was now considering university, and thankfully was able to get a scholarship that would cover some of the tuition. The two girls were no longer in private school, but were doing great in a Catholic high school around the corner from where they now lived. This was a great school with a good reputation, and both girls were admitted to the school's International Baccalaureate program and doing exceptionally well. Anne was happy with the girls' progress and their easy transition into the school environment. She had never considered taking them out of private school, but after being forced into this decision she was surprised at how well it was working out.

Anne and Robert had split their assets, and still had some shared outstanding debt they were working on. Rob had moved to a rented apartment. It seemed the financial stress for so many years had slowly eaten away at their relationship and in the end had been one of the factors contributing to their split.

COACH'S MESSAGE

Consider becoming a champion to your kids and more than a just a role model. Why would we want them to go out into society believing that life is so easy? It isn't. Life can be hard, and only those who are willing to work for what they want will prosper and become financially secure as they age.

We live in a society that for the most part believes in entitlement—hence, growing debt and shrinking retirement savings.

You are not alone if you are like Anne and Rob. This seems to be a trend among the upper-middle class.

"I deserve to buy this."

"I need to have this car because of my job title."

"My kids need to have more than I did."

"It's a really great deal. I should buy now."

People have lost the ability to evaluate everything they do in terms of the bigger picture. Most people today are far too optimistic about their future, believing it will all work out. Some even believe their kids have a duty to support them financially in old age. A client once said their kids had been told countless times they would have to help their parents when they retired since they were not going to have enough money. Please, don't knowingly put this burden on your children. Rise to the challenge of being self-sufficient in your retirement. Isn't that what you are trying to teach your kids—to be self-sufficient? We want our children to go out into the world, get a good job, buy a home, raise a family, and have a good life. You want them to be successful and productive members of society when they leave home. Why would you put the burden on them to be your financial provider because you were not prudent enough with your money during your working years? We need to show our children the value of saving for the future or they won't have one either.

Have a plan to get to your goal, and create a burning desire inside you to keep moving in the right direction to reach it. Don't think you are alone in this struggle. Seek the advice of professionals who want you to succeed and who will provide you with ideas to help you get there. Become empowered and, most of all, have full buy-in by all participants, your spouse, kids, even your dog. Do not think you can do this on your own as a "lone wolf." It doesn't work. All family members need to be on board.

Now, I know you might get some resistance from the kids, but remember: you are the parent, and you are going to set the example of responsibility and financial resolve. Don't worry—they are more adaptable than you think. You might even find that, after time, they might even be happy with the changes.

Keep focused on the benefits. Both you and your spouse have to want your goal. You will have no one else to blame other than yourself if you reach retirement with debt and not enough saved. You can do it.

SELF-EMPLOYED PROFESSIONALS WITH HIGH LIFESTYLES: DR. BROWN AND KAREN BROWN

Some self-employed professionals, such as doctors, dentists, and lawyers, live far beyond their means, believing they will be able to sell their practice at the end of their working years and easily finance their retirement from those funds. It is important to remember that there will always be changes to your business through the years, and you should never get too comfortable. Sometimes a very successful practice will experience a reduction in patients or clients due to changes in the economy and the demographics of a changing business area.

Dr. Brown had a dental practice in a mid-sized town for over twenty years and was now fifty-six. When I asked him if he planned to retire in nine years at sixty-five, he replied that he would never be able to retire, and I soon would find out why. The once small town had seen a huge increase in new housing developments in the past ten years, and had grown from a sleepy place to a hustling, bustling new urban place. The population had grown by a whopping 56.5% as more families looked for affordable housing just outside the big city. Land shortage in big cities is always a problem, and if young families prefer a small detached home over an apartment condo, they find that their money goes further when they move out of the greater metropolitan areas. Because of a new commuter train that now serviced the town, more young families were making it their home.

This sounded like great news for anyone with an already-established dental business, but it actually turned out to be the exact opposite for this client. With more population came more competition from younger and more forward-thinking entrepreneurs. With no defined legislation to regulate new dentists, the small town became saturated with new dental offices opening up on what seemed like every street corner.

Dr. Brown was used to working nine to five, Monday to Friday, and his patients would take time off work to go to a dental appointment. Not anymore. His competition soon found a niche market and capitalized on it. Now, there were lots of dental offices in town with younger doctors open from 7:00 A.M. to 9:00 P.M. and even offering appointments on the weekends.

Unfortunately, Dr. Brown's business suffered considerably year over year, but, of course, his lifestyle did not. He was married with three girls, now all moved out. Two were married and one was in her last year of university. Dr. Brown and his wife Karen lived in another town only thirty minutes away. Their home was worth approximately $900,000. They had a mortgage of $296,000, a secured line of credit fully drawn for $338,000, $57,600 in credit card debt, and an overdraft of $12,200 that never got paid off. They also had two car lease payments for $900 and $480 per month. Dr. Brown still had approximately $400,000 in business loans, and was considering expanding his practice, which would add another $100,000.

Two years ago, he decided to downsize to one secretary and one hygienist, but now did not know what to do next. Should he expand

and take on a higher business loan with no guarantee of increased business? Or should he cut his losses and liquidate the business? He believed that if he sold his practice, he would barely make enough to cover his existing business loans, and could not expect to reap much of a profit from the sale. His annual income was now $83,000, a far cry from the $290,000–$330,000 he was used to making many years ago. His wife also worked, making $138,000 as a human resources manager of an accounting firm in the city, and would receive a pension at retirement. Their personal debt totalled $722,800, and they had approximately $320,000 in savings. Their net worth was $497,000. A change to either Dr. Brown's business or their lifestyle had to be considered, since continuing on this path would soon lead them to retirement with more debt and little to live on.

SO WHAT DID THEY DO?

When we sat down together it was very important for Dr. Brown and Karen to really open up about where they wanted to be in the next few years and how they planned to keep funding their lifestyle into retirement. It was necessary to understand the dynamics of their incomes and how we would begin planning the incremental steps to resolving their financial situation. Most people will not want to lower their standard of living at retirement, and the biggest risk to this couple would be if they chose not to do anything to improve their current finances. It was necessary to seek a solution now, while there was still time to make course corrections to improve.

Many people become mired by indecision, and end up doing nothing to correct their finances before they retire. Be careful not to be one of these unfortunate people who finds themselves after many years in an even worse financial situation with more debt and a huge lifestyle adjustment at retirement.

Instead of dwelling on the misfortunes of the past ten years, we wanted these clients to seize the opportunities they now had before them. Dr. Brown had some great knowledge about the town, since he had worked there for over twenty years and had seen first-hand the expansion and development. He knew where the good areas of town were, and had more insight about local economics and new developments than did any newcomers. We wanted to capitalize on this. Currently they had $634,000 owing on their home in the form of a mortgage and line of credit. Add on the credit card debt and overdraft at a whopping 21%, and we were up to $703,800. This had to be reduced. The two car leases were also a drain on their monthly cash flow, and it was decided that we should buy out Karen's car to eliminate the payment and now own the vehicle. This would add another $19,000, making their total debt $722,800.

We suggested a two-pronged approach to tackle the business and personal debts. Although this solution sounded extreme at first, they were very happy with it, and planned to make it happen. First, we wanted them to sell their home and downsize to something new. Because the town was growing, we could count on the new purchase doubling in value in eight to twelve years. It was important to buy new and to use Dr. Brown's knowledge of the town to find the best location for our new asset purchase. We wanted the Browns to begin thinking of this solution as an investment in their future, and so it was important for them to pick a property based on its potential resale value in the near future.

The Browns' home would sell for approximately $910,000, and after paying off all the debt of $722,800 and the real estate fees and taxes they could expect to have a net surplus of approximately $128,900. We wanted them to purchase a new home in town for $600,000. With a $120,000 down payment, they would have an estimated new mortgage of $480,000. With no debt other than the new mortgage, together with lower property taxes and no home improvement costs, this purchase could instantly create more monthly cash flow. It would now be easier to live on their combined incomes, and they could work at paying down this mortgage and perhaps even try to have it paid off by the time they retire.

By moving to a new home in a very popular community, they could feel confident that, once they reached retirement, their investment should have doubled. The home they sold had already reached its maximum value and would soon need updating and expensive maintenance costs to ensure the value increased nominally every year. With the three girls now having moved out and making their own lives, this was a good time to cash out on their primary residence and use the funds to eliminate their high-interest debts.

To address Dr. Brown's business, we talked at length about his thoughts on expansion and competition. The old phrase "if you can't beat them, join them" was exactly what we proposed. Dr. Brown's practice was located in an excellent part of town, with high traffic, good parking, and in a very trendy, up-and-coming area. We wanted him to consider expanding his office and allowing another dentist to buy into his practice. This would help with the expansion costs and also potentially lower his business loan. We felt this would be a win-win situation for both a new dentist and our client.

A new dentist could now buy into a very successful location that was already set up, had modern equipment, trained staff, and an existing client base on which to build. With a new, eager dentist willing to work extended hours to build more patients, Dr. Brown's business could expand and compete more easily with other new dental offices in town.

TWENTY-FOUR MONTHS LATER

The Browns made some big changes to their lifestyle. They took charge of their lives and replaced negative thoughts with positive ones. They believed in their plan and moved out of their old comfortable ways and into a new state of control and power. The Browns sold their home and bought a beautiful, brand-new house in the same town for $602,000, and really enjoyed picking all their new options and colours. They successfully cut their debt by almost 50%, and now seemed to be even more motivated to eliminate their new mortgage by retirement. They planned to keep their monthly payments the same as they were when they had double the debt, and by taking advantage of the low mortgage rates they could expect to have their new mortgage paid off in only eleven years. Due to the location and the demographics of this new urban town, it was expected that their purchase would most likely double in value to approximately $1,150,000 once the mortgage was paid.

Dr. Brown took our advice to diversify his business, and we were thrilled to hear about his new business success. He was able to expand his office to accommodate two new dentists who bought into his business for $200,000 each. This $400,000 paid off his old business loans and the expansion cost him $100,000. With a much larger office, he was able to hire back his old staff. The two new dentists had committed to an advertising budget, and were bringing in new patients. This was a great success story. When talking to Dr. Brown about all the changes to his business, you could feel the enthusiasm in his voice. Now his practice was moving in the right direction. Instead of folding his business and giving up, he had completely turned things around and injected new life into his practice and his future. He had lowered his business debt to only $100,000 and now could sell his patient practice to his partners once he retired. The plan was to pay off the business loan over the next ten years and continue to grow his practice until his retirement.

The Browns' investments totalling $320,000 were distributed in a laddered fixed income portfolio, and would net $553,000 at retirement. Their home would be worth approximately $1,200,000, and the sale of Dr. Brown's business partnership was projected to net $300,000. Their plan at retirement was to move to a much less expensive rural community and begin to travel once a year and just enjoy a slower pace of life. Their net worth would be $2,053,000, and they would still have Karen's pension and Old Age Security for both. The future was good. They had created it themselves by having the courage to take charge and make the changes they needed.

COACH'S MESSAGE

Most people would not have made the changes that Dr. Brown and his wife did to sell their home and expand their business. However, if you are lucky enough to know about an urban area that is growing quickly and becoming more popular, it just makes good business sense to buy into this location and capitalize on the gain.

People have lost the ability to see everything they do in terms of the bigger picture. Instead, many refuse to make changes to their current poor financial situations. They wonder why it never worked out as they had planned, and then quietly join the ranks of all those miserable at retirement because the world just didn't give them the opportunities they thought they deserved.

You must take control of your finances and your life, and start creating your own opportunities and advantages. Look around at your life and see if there are any ways for you to capitalize on your own knowledge and circumstances. Just as these clients did, start stacking the odds in your favour and take back your financial future.

In the business world, companies can't afford to beat around the bush. They have business analysts and accountants who keep the company always moving forward. If they don't make enough money to run the business, they cut jobs, sell part of the business, or downsize. It is the same at home and in your own life. Remove your emotional attachment to your things and your debt, and become like a business analyst reviewing your own finances. Tell it like it is and be honest with yourself. Remember, your biggest risk is to do nothing. Only you can guarantee your future. Don't be afraid to get started.

AFFLUENT CLIENTS ARE NOT AFRAID OF DEBT, BUT THEY SHOULD BE: CAROLINE

The closer we are to retirement, the stronger become our feelings and behaviours toward preparing for our later years. What if you are now at the retirement age, but not yet retired? Caroline was seventy-one, a business owner, socialite, and proud mother of two very successful sons and the grandmother of five lovely grandchildren. She had always been used to a very high lifestyle, and had never had to manage her money, choosing to let her advisors and accountants handle her affairs.

She was the eldest daughter of a very wealthy family, and enjoyed a privileged childhood. She was educated at the finest schools, and moved in high society social circles with other affluent people. After her third divorce and poor investment decisions, she found herself in a situation that she and her accountant had been sweeping under the rug for a very long time. Caroline had over $1,965,000 in credit card debt, lines of credit, and personal loans. She always said to friends that she did not have a mortgage, but little did they know that she had every other debt you could think of. Her secured line of credit, $1,450,000, was maxed out. She had opted for interest-only loans for the past fifteen years, and had not made any attempt to pay down the principal balances. Creative accounting and the desire for more cash flow made it necessary to lower monthly expenses, resulting in the plan to make interest-only payments.

This is a lender's dream! The interest that she had paid over the past fifteen years was $1,249,924, and when I showed this to Caroline I was not surprised to see that this did not faze her. By never paying off the principal, you never learn how to manage your money, and the banks feed off you until they finally say, "Enough. Okay, we are calling the loans. Please pay up." Now what?

Revolving credit can be called at any time, and most clients fail to realize that they will have to pay it off sometime. Most clients would be unable to rest for even a minute with large overwhelming debt loads, whereas many very affluent clients are simply not worried and have become desensitized. They are lulled into a sense of complacency, and have tremendous peer pressure to maintain a certain high lifestyle to move among their social circles.

Always thinking of monthly cash flow is very important, but not at the expense of never reducing your debt. Caroline was lucky that interest rates had been on a downward trend for the past ten years, but if we were to have even a nominal increase in the rates, it could be catastrophic. With every spike in future rates, clients will find themselves unprepared for the consequences. Some may even find themselves backed into a financial corner, perhaps permanently. It was necessary for Caroline to make some changes to secure her future for the next twenty-five years, and she was finally ready to do so. It was time to stop making interest-only payments and try to make a dent in reducing her loans.

Let's look at the difference between an interest-only scenario and a principal-plus-interest solution over a period of five years. We will use a basic example of, say, $2,000,000. When you choose to pay only interest, the banks will charge you a slightly higher rate on the loan amount than on a mortgage loan, which favours a principal-plus-interest payment.

SCENARIO 1: INTEREST-ONLY PAYMENTS

On $2,000,000, the interest rate was prime + 0.50%. Prime at the time of this deal was 3%, so the rate was 3.5%. If the prime rate were to go up or down, the rate would fluctuate but would always be at prime + 0.50%.

Remember, the rate is always subject to change at the lender's discretion, and will be outlined in writing when you sign. The rate in this example is a very good one on a secured line of credit compared with past rates of prime + 1.00% or prime + 1.50%.

The monthly commitment for this loan would be $5,835. The total interest paid over the next five years would be $350,000, and the balance would remain at $2,000,000.

SCENARIO 2: PRINCIPAL-PLUS-INTEREST PAYMENTS

The interest rate on a variable open mortgage for this loan was offered at 3.00%, just half a percentage point lower than in Scenario 1. This was not a significant rate reduction, but we recommended the client choose a variable product because the accrued interest is calculated based on the amount outstanding each month, similar to the line of credit option above.

The monthly commitment for this loan would be $9,346, a significant increase of $3,511 in the client's budget. However, we knew that the client could afford this payment, and we wanted to demonstrate how she would actually make money by choosing this option. Over five years, she would pay an extra $210,660 due to the increased monthly payment ($3,511 x 60 months). After five years, the outstanding balance on the $2,000,000 loan would be $1,673,624, a difference of $326,376. Why the lower balance? If we only made extra payments of $210,660, why was the balance reduced by $326,276?

Let's compare the two examples—here is what we found. The line of credit at $2,000,000 with a lump sum payment of $210,660 would ensure a balance of $1,789,340. Still, with scenario 2, there was a greater difference of $115,716 paid down to lower the outstanding balance. The reason this plan works every time is that, unlike a conventional mortgage where the interest is calculated annually or semi-annually, the interest on a variable loan is calculated monthly. The product automatically recalibrates the interest based on the outstanding balance each month. While the monthly payment does not change, the percentages to principal and interest do, and are therefore adjusted after each payment. That means that, with each monthly payment, more goes to principal and less goes to interest, constantly adjusting and working with you to fast-track your debt. It is almost like dollar-cost averaging, but in reverse. Simply put, you are paying down your principal faster.

Let's look it another way. If I were to promise you that if you gave me $210,660 to invest over the next five years, I could secure your capital and provide you with a profit of $115,716, would you do it? This would mean your investment would grow to $326,376 in five years, an increase of 155% on your investment. Would you do it now?

You know you would, right? So why are you not choosing to invest in yourself by paying off your debt?

By using a collateral charge as a platform for this product, you can pay down the debt and then draw it out again without requalifying. A typical mortgage is not the same thing. With a mortgage, once you pay it down, the portion that you have paid cannot be used again unless you requalify for a new loan. With a collateral charge, this step is eliminated.

SO WHAT DID SHE DO?

We approved Caroline for a $2,000,000 collateral charge at the prime rate of 3.00% with a balance of $1,965,000. We set up a loan segment to be calculated monthly, but requested she pay principal and interest to ensure we could make a sizable dent in her debt. Using our five-year benchmark, she would have a balance owing of $1,616,335. Because she had been approved and agreed to the collateral charge of $2,000,000, this meant that she now had $383,665 in available credit to draw on if she needed it. We advise clients to pay down their debt continually so that, if in the future they need the additional funds for an unforeseen necessity, they have it available and do not have to reapply with the banks.

A collateral charge has no term or renewal, and is considered to be a lifetime product that clients can use and manage on their own. Within the charge you pay only for what you owe, which means unused available credit has no cost until it is used. The only time a client would need to requalify with the bank is if they moved to another lending institution or requested a higher limit. Most collateral charges are also portable, and allow the client to transfer them to another property as long as the new property is valued at the same or higher amount than the approved charge limit. If the client is downsizing, the charge can still be transferred, but the limit would be reduced. No requalification is needed, and there is usually a nominal transfer or port fee.

When I presented this solution to Caroline, she was motivated to make a change, but wanted her business manager and accountant to review the numbers. I knew both of them very well. Caroline's accountant did not see the point in changing things. While he agreed that no debt is good debt, he believed that it was not necessary for her to increase her payments to pay down the principal and lower the loan amounts. We agreed that the debt eventually would be paid off once the client died through the sale of her estate, but what happens if the client lives longer than she anticipates? By paying down the loans, you not only stop the banks from making more money on you; you also create an opportunity for equity takeouts in the future.

It turned out, when we had a few more discussions with Caroline's advisors, that her accountant firmly believed in not paying off debts to increase monthly cash flow because he also was heavily leveraged and used this method in his own personal finances. This was not good—however, he was not our client, so we could not comment.

Just as a side note: If you are overweight, wanting to get thin and healthy, and you have a FAT doctor telling you, "you're fine, you don't need to lose weight," what do you do? RUN!! Get someone who is not in the same position as you and doesn't want you to stay there so that they have company.

Because Caroline's accountant had a very similar situation, he always advised her to keep her cash flow higher by paying interest only. Many affluent clients have advisors who have been with their family for decades. Consider getting some fresh new advice if your situation is not improving year over year. Please, talk to an advisor who has only your best interests in mind, not their own. Bottom line, it is you who makes the final decision and will have to "pay the piper" at the end.

We wanted Caroline to rein in her spending and completely review her financial circumstances. By becoming more involved and not turning a blind eye toward your finances, you begin to change for the better. Once you start seeing where all your money is going and what is coming in, you begin to appreciate the changes you can make and enjoy watching the savings grow every month. Caroline had never done this, and had left her finances up to her accountant or her previous husbands.

It was quite difficult at first for Caroline to take on this new role, but I saw a change in her that I had never seen before. She had always been a very high-powered businesswoman with great negotiating skills, and it was easy for the average person to feel intimidated when she spoke. Caroline decided to attack her finances as she would when she took on a new business project and began making changes. Taking control seemed to empower Caroline even more, and helped her to move to a more calming life space that now had certainty and direction for the future.

Having agreed to the collateral charge for $2,000,000, we were able to provide Caroline with increased flexibility and security. She most likely would not be approved for any increases since she was already in her seventies, but this really did not matter for her future plans. Since the charge has no term or renewal, she would be able to make use of it for as long as she lived, and by paying down the debt she ensured future room was available for any necessary cash withdrawals. Furthermore, by creating a cap on the debt at $2,000,000 through the collateral charge, we now have easy estate planning and know that the debt will never exceed this amount. We can plan investment strategies around this controlled amount, and budget for its dissolution by the estate at the time of death.

COACH'S MESSAGE

The less time we have remaining in our working years, the more activity and greater resolve this creates to increase savings and lower debt loads. But don't wait until the very end. You must plan if you want to retire wealthy and debt-free. Having a lot of money tied up in assets means nothing if it is burdened with extensive obligations. Consider exploring new ideas, and free yourself from the old ways of the past. If you have an advisor or accountant who is holding you back, consider getting a second opinion. You deserve it.

Caroline's solution can also apply to smaller mortgages and loans. Paying principal and interest every month and having your product adjust monthly based on the lower outstanding balance creates a "true pay for what you owe" product. The interest is adjusted downward, and the allotment to the principal increases each and every month. This is possible in a variable mortgage format that mimics a line of credit and is best used in a collateral charge platform. Fixed mortgages calculate their interest annually or semi-annually and therefore will not offer the same reducing effect over the long term. It is best to review your mortgage or loan setup and begin to become more aware of how much money you are really spending on interest over time.

By using this solution, you can create a cushion of security in the collateral charge that can be drawn down again if needed in the future. The charge remains the same, and because there is no renewal in the future, the client is free to pay it off, draw it down as needed, or switch to interest only in the future if required. The client has complete flexibility and control to manage his or her own financial situation. This solution will always make sense for estate planning purposes.

Many new products are now available to encourage clients to take control of their own financial future. For the right client, this is freedom. Having the flexibility to change the product offers clients the opportunity to plan for their future and stimulates new ideas to dissolve debt and plan for retirement. We need to begin to think outside the box and put ourselves in solutions that work with us to provide a lasting effect on debt reduction. I encourage you to explore new lending instruments and speak to advisors who provide innovative and creative ways to get you where you want to go. Start creating your own financial destiny to increase your net worth by reducing your overall indebtedness. With a few simple changes and a little effort, you will be well on your way to being wealthy.

USING RENTAL PROPERTIES TO INCREASE WEALTH:

Cheryl and James

LIFE HAS A WAY OF MAKING SURE EVERYONE EXPERIENCES "SOME KIND of challenge," and Cheryl and James were no different than most. They had dealt with the constant challenges of raising three kids, and Cheryl had recovered from breast cancer in her thirties. Now that their kids were in their teens, they thought life might be easier. They were not prepared for what came next. James was making $190,000 a year, and had worked his way up the corporate ladder to become part of the executive team of a large Fortune 500 company, only to find himself squeezed out after a twenty-year tenure. It took over a year for James to find another executive position with a much smaller company. His income and ego had been considerably bruised, but as a couple they were determined to set things right again.

James was fifty-one and now had an income of $130,000. Cheryl, an elementary teacher, was forty-nine and her income was $52,000. Their home was valued at $600,000 and they had a mortgage of $335,000. Their investment portfolio had been supplemented by the severance package and now totalled $345,000. James did not have a pension at his new employer, but anticipated working until sixty-five, so we had only fourteen years left to ensure their finances were in order. Cheryl could expect a pension from the school board.

They had purchased two rental properties seven years ago. On the advice of their financial planner, they financed the properties using secured lines of credit. This strategy ensured a lower payment, since they were responsible only for the interest, and this method made it very easy to write off the payments from the monthly statements. Almost all advisors and most accountants recommend this method so that the interest is clearly defined when used to lower your marginal tax rate. Declaring the rental properties on your tax return forces you to add the rental income to your employment income, but in turn provides you with numerous tax write-offs. You will be able to write off all expenses for your rental properties, including cleaning supplies, property taxes, gas and mileage travelling to and from the properties, maintenance, loss of rent, and, of course, the mortgage interest.

I disagree with the use of credit lines for investment properties, since the whole idea of owning the rental is to have the property go up in value while the tenant pays down the debt through the monthly rent. You absolutely want the mortgage to decrease and eventually get paid off so that, when you sell the property, you will have a larger return on your investment. Preserving the original balance with the use of an interest-only line of credit further puts you at risk if the housing market declines. Frankly, if you must use a line of credit, rather than a mortgage, because you wish to increase cash flow, then you probably have not got it set up properly. As you will see with Cheryl and James, once you change your situation to start working for you, investment rentals can become a money-making machine that guarantees your future wealth.

In addition to their mortgage, Cheryl and James had a line of credit on their current home for $143,000 and a line of credit on each rental: one for $251,000 and another for $242,000. The rents were easily covering the interest payments, condo fees, and property taxes, but the balance on the lines never changed. During the previous couple of years, making interest-only payments was fine, but now it was time to make sure these loans were decreasing. They had an additional $68,000 in credit card debt accumulated over the eighteen months when James was out of work, and with the challenges of helping with the upcoming university education of three teens, together with the much lower income, they were finding it tough. Both rental properties were now over twelve years old, and therefore could be expected to go up only gradually with market trends.

The clients did not want to sell their rental properties, but wanted to try to buy more in the future. However, the debt load seemed never-ending, and they were not sure how to get to retirement debt-free. The uncertainty in the stock market made them uneasy to invest any more in their mutual funds, and they were not happy with the returns or fees. They believed that the rentals would diversify their investment portfolio with tangible assets. Their current net worth was $525,000.

SO WHAT DID THEY DO?

When I met with Cheryl and James, I knew that their situation could be easily modified to produce a money-making investment solution. However, I needed them to be open to a new way of lending. All banks offer the same thing—mortgages and lines of credit—and I wanted them to consider an alternative strategy that we have been using in our private banking divisions for years. Simply doing the same thing from now to retirement was not going to deliver the results these clients wanted, so I asked them to consider the methods used by our affluent clients to enhance their finances.

The first thing we needed to do was to determine the value of each rental property and determine how much of their $143,000 line of credit on their primary residence was used to purchase the rentals (initial deposit or down payments) and how much was just extra personal expenses.

Here is what we determined.

Rental 1:
Purchase price = $315,000
Line of credit = $251,000 + $64,000
Market value = $398,000

Rental 2:
Purchase price = $304,000
Line of credit = $242,000 + $62,000
Market value = $381,500

The $64,000 and $62,000 were the original down payments made when the clients purchased the rentals, and could now be deducted from the $143,000 line of credit on their primary home and placed back on the rental properties. This is called an equity alignment. The property value of each rental had now increased and could be easily restructured to incorporate the original 100% purchase price. Adding these back, it was now easy to determine that approximately $17,000 had been used for personal expenses on their line of credit.

MORE ABOUT A COLLATERAL CHARGE

A collateral charge will become more popular as more people discover the flexibility and ease of this lending instrument, and we decided to use this product for Cheryl and James. All the big banks offer a variation on the 100% collateral charge, so it is a good idea to understand fully each of their offerings. It is a great tool for investors or clients wanting to purchase rental properties, and can be used effectively for tax efficiency. The product is called a "charge" because it is secured on a property for 100% of its appraised value at the time of setup. The client signs for the full value of the property, but will have access only to 80%, thereby meeting the guidelines of a conventional lending platform. The collateral charge has no term or renewal, and the client can set it up and use it for as long as he or she owns the property, therefore ensuring no additional title fees or legal costs. Herein lies one of its true benefits.

Because the client signs for the full value of the property, there is available room for future equity takeouts as the value increases over time, and this built-in equity can be used as future lending availability. Another added benefit is that the charge is approved and set up only one time, and the client no longer has to renew or change banks at the end of a typical mortgage term. Within the charge, the client can easily manipulate the product to take advantage of special rate promotions or leverage lending.

Most big banks offer this product with the flexibility of up to ten different lending segments, so that each segment can run independently from the others. All segments can have different rates and terms that can be easily changed at the client's discretion. A collateral charge is perfect for someone who wants to purchase rental properties, and is used by our affluent clients exclusively.

When you purchase an investment property, the collateral charge will be set up for 100% of the purchase price. The federal government now mandates that rentals cannot be mortgaged for more than 80%, and this is fine for this product. If you wish to write off the full 100% of the purchase, it is always recommended to have a collateral charge on your primary residence to establish a separate segment for the 20% down payment portion. Most banks will label each segment for you to ensure that, come tax time, one can clearly differentiate between a personal mortgage segment and a rental segment. Here is an example.

Let's say that you wish to purchase a rental property for $300,000 and want to use the down payment for the purchase ($60,000) from the equity in your home. Let's also assume that your primary residence is valued at $500,000 and you have a personal mortgage of $200,000. Here is how the two charges would be set up.

Value of your home = $500,000
Collateral charge signed for $500,000
Initial release of available credit = $400,000 (80%)

Segment 1:
Primary mortgage = $200,000, fixed, variable, or line of credit
Segment 2:
Rental property (20%) = $60,000 (tax write-off), fixed, variable or line of credit

<u>Segment 3:</u>
Line of credit (leftover available credit) = $140,000
Balance = $0.00 (no payments)

Value of your new rental property = $300,000
Collateral charge signed for $300,000
Initial release of available credit = $240,000 (80%)

<u>Segment 1:</u>
Rental mortgage (80%) = $240,000 (tax write-off)

So now you have two charges, one on your primary residence and one on the rental. The full purchase of the rental ($300,000) is spread across both properties, and instead of amalgamating the $60,000 down payment into a new refinanced mortgage, as most people do, we have kept it separated in an individual segment. By doing this, we have clearly defined the purchase, and can easily demonstrate to the CRA the full 100% value to be used as a tax write-off.

As your properties go up in value, you can take advantage of this increased equity without the trouble of refinancing and legal fees. In our example, once the rental property increases in value to $375,000, the client could access the full collateral charge of $300,000 (still within the 80% loan-to-value ratio for the banks based on the higher appraised value). These new funds can be used to purchase another rental, pay down the rental segment on your primary residence, or even as a lump sum to pay down your primary mortgage.

NOW LET'S GET BACK TO OUR CLIENTS' STRATEGY.
For Cheryl and James, we wanted to put a collateral charge on both rentals as well as on their primary residence. The values of both rentals had

increased substantially since their purchase, and we were able to set up a segment on each rental that was the same as the original purchase price. These new segments were not put into lines of credit, but set up in a mortgage format so that the rental income would pay down the balances in a predetermined principal and interest payment each month. Choosing to pay only interest allows you to take advantage of a smaller payment, but your loan never decreases. Always try to stay away from lines of credit, since they are ultimately designed to help the banks get richer.

By refinancing the two rental properties, we were able to put the original purchase price back on the property because of the increase in value. This would make it seamless. Here is how we set up Cheryl and James's new financial solution.

RENTAL 1:
Appraised value and collateral charge limit = $398,000

Segment 1:
Fixed mortgage = $315,000 (includes $251,000 + $64,000 from line of credit)

Segment 2:
Available credit $3,400 (80% of $398,000 = $318,400)

RENTAL 2:
Appraised value and collateral charge limit = $380,500

Segment 1:
Fixed mortgage = $304,000 (includes $242,000 + $62,000 from line of credit)

Segment 2:
Available credit $400 (80% of 380,500 = $304,400)

PRIMARY RESIDENCE:
Appraised value and collateral charge = $600,000

Segment 1:
Fixed mortgage = $420,000 (includes $17,000 balance on line of credit + $68,000 credit card debt + $335,000 mortgage)

Segment 2:
Available credit = $60,000 (80% of $600,000 = $480,000)

This new solution on all three properties instantly brought clarity to Cheryl and James and provided them with the future ability to withdraw the equity from the rental properties without refinancing again. These future equity takeouts could be used to make lump-sum payments on their primary mortgage to ensure it is paid off by retirement. Keeping the investment properties provides a growing asset that will continue to be paid off by the rental income, while still providing tax incentives.

Keeping on track and without incurring any new debt, Cheryl and James could expect to have paid off their primary mortgage within the fourteen years until James retired. Using the Finance Tracker and Daily Cash Journal, these clients could rein in their spending and continue to stay focused on debt reduction.

At retirement, rental 1 potentially would still have a balance of $127,000, while rental 2 would have a balance of $112,000. If they chose to sell the rental properties at retirement, they could expect to pocket approximately $556,805 from rental 1 and $541,960 from rental 2 after capital gains tax, real estate, and legal fees. It is advisable to liquidate one a year in retirement to minimize the amount paid in taxes. Here is how we estimated the projection of return on the investment properties.

Rental 1:

$788,300	Estimated value in 15 years (based on 2–4% increase per year)
(127,000)	Less mortgage outstanding
(31,500)	Less real estate fees at 4%
(2,000)	Less legal fees
(70,995)	Less capital gains tax on $236,650 at 30% marginal tax rate
$556,805	Profit

Rental 2:

$753,600	Estimated value in 15 years (based on 2–4% increase per year)
(112,000)	Less mortgage outstanding
(30,200)	Less real estate fees at 4%
(2,000)	Less legal fees
(67,440)	Less capital gains tax on $224,800 at 30% marginal tax rate
$541,960	Profit

At retirement Cheryl and James could expect to have a net worth of $3,055,400. They could easily continue to live in their home, and once they sell the rental properties and add the proceeds to their investment portfolio, they could expect to retire on approximately $1,867,000, plus government pension plans and Cheryl's school board pension. Their original investment portfolio of $345,000 was put into a laddered compounding fixed income investment structure that would be worth $768,246 after fourteen years. They were definitely going to be very comfortable at retirement, and were well on their way to being very wealthy.

COACH'S MESSAGE

Buying rental properties and dealing with the maintenance and constant issues with tenants is not for everyone. Most people do not want the added debt, stress, or worry in their already full lives. With both parents working and the demands of children, it is easy to see how many people would not even think of owning investment properties. There is also the added stress of the property market decreasing or falling into recession at the time you wish to sell. With all this in mind, I still must tell you that owning real estate is one of the oldest ways to increase your wealth. There are many very wealthy people today who have never invested in the stock market but have made their fortunes through real estate.

One of the biggest drains on a person's income is taxes: taxes from your employer, on things you purchase, and on your home. If you are looking for an alternative investment that offers tax advantages while still providing a solid return on a tangible asset, rental properties are your answer.

If you are considering buying investment properties as Cheryl and James did, always make sure you are preapproved and that your budget can take the unexpected added expenses if a tenant doesn't pay or a property is vacant. Ensure you set up a principal and interest payment structure to have your rental income always paying down the outstanding debt. Start small, and remember that the benefits of owning real estate as a long-term investment almost always provide great future wealth.

There are three things to consider when buying an investment property. Follow these easy steps in the chapter that follows, and it won't be long till you become a millionaire, too.

Good luck!

THREE KEY COMPONENTS TO PURCHASING RENTAL PROPERTIES

1. DO YOUR HOMEWORK: DEMOGRAPHICS, LOCATION, AGE, POTENTIAL TO RENT/SELL

Always be sure of what you are buying. Make sure that you are purchasing a property that can be easily sold in the future and is in an area that will continually increase in value.

Watch out for condo apartments. Most people buy condos because they are cheaper, easier to maintain, and are usually the most uncomplicated to rent. With this in mind, however, if there are a lot of rentals in the building, the values will not increase as much as a townhouse or small detached home. Some big banks have even banned mortgage lending on some condominium developments in major cities due to the overall high percentage of rentals in the buildings. Always check with your lender to see if there are any restrictions on the condominium you wish to purchase before you firm up your deal.

Consider buying investment properties that are newer. The greatest appreciation in property value will be in the first five to seven years. If you choose to buy an older property that has an existing tenant, always check the history. There are restrictions on rental increases if you purchase a property that was previously rented prior to 1991. Again, do your homework, and make sure it is a good investment for your future.

2. REDUCE STRESS: PROPERTY MANAGER, ACCOUNTANT, LEGAL ADVISOR, REALTOR

Consider getting a service to handle your rental properties. Most property management companies will guarantee occupancy from their pool of renters, and can help clients with high-cost executive rentals. They provide services on how to prepare your property, and can negotiate lease agreements with tenants and corporate relocation companies.

Having a property manager is similar to having an investment advisor. An investment advisor handles all the details of your stock and investment portfolio, while a property manager handles all the details of your properties and any questions and complaints of your tenants. Both are there to manage your assets so that you can have less involvement but still enjoy the gain of an appreciating portfolio.

If a full-service property management company is not for you, there are many internet services that can help you advertise your property and help find potential tenants. When doing it on your own, you will now have to do what the property managers would do to screen potential tenants. Ask for references, obtain a credit report, and consider having the tenants fill out a detailed application to determine if they are a good fit for you and your property.

Talk to your accountant and your lawyer before you purchase to understand the rental restrictions and laws for landlords and tenants in your area. Always be informed and make sure to research all the facets of your new investment so that you can eliminate potential surprises in the future.

3. PROTECT YOUR FUTURE: PROPERTY AND DEBT INSURANCE

Most people will not want to get insurance on their rental properties, but instead will say, "If I die, my family will sell it." This is not a good answer. Insurance provides protection against loss, and should always be applied when you take on more risk. The amount of insurance should, at a minimum, equal the amount of debt that your family would be left with should you die. The rental could then provide monthly income and ensure that the property would not have to be sold in a "fire sale" to pay for taxes, expenses, or unqualifiable debt.

If one spouse dies, the property will pass tax free to the surviving spouse. If, however, you both die, the properties will pass to your estate and be considered as a deemed disposal, subject to income taxes, probate taxes, and all capital gains taxes. Without insurance, your heirs could be left with very little inheritance after the government takes its share of all your assets. Don't "nickel and dime" your family's quality of life or your children's future. The cost of insurance is not worth the loss of your hard-earned asset and investment property when you die unprotected.

In the previous client story about Cheryl and James, we touched on new ways to explore rental properties to increase your long-term wealth. There are many new options and creative lending initiatives that will get you the results you seek, so don't be afraid to ask your advisor or private banker. It can get very exciting planning new ways to boost your retirement savings, but remember that while your emotions build visions and goals, they should not drive your financial decisions if they are not methodically planned out and budgeted. You should always balance risk and return using a planned, results-based strategy built for today's market, your demographics, and, most of all, you and your family.

Become your own personal financial planner. Get involved, get inspired, and do your homework.

WHAT THE BANKS LOOK FOR WHEN LENDING

There are three main levels of lending in the United States and Canada: A, B, and C lenders. The A lenders are the largest banks, which have most of the market share across the country. They are the movers and shakers of the banking world and always tend to move in tandem when raising and lowering rates. Their stock is traded worldwide, and they are generally considered the foundational backbone of our financial system.

Their lending practices are virtually the same across all channels, and if you are declined by one of them, you most probably will be declined by them all.

The B lenders are the smaller banks and credit unions. They normally specialize in clients with unique lending requirements, and provide products to clients who do not fit the typical credit criteria. These lenders are an alternative source for clients, and they usually partner with all the big banks for spinoff business.

In recent years, the A lenders have become very creative in ensuring that they do not lose clients when they decline a deal. By partnering with B lenders, the big banks have found that they can now give the client an approval through their alternative lending channels or alternative mortgage services (AMS). This approval is from the partnering B lender, but because of this alignment, the client will still get all the personal banking services and promotional offers from the big bank or A lender. The A lender receives a partnering fee from the smaller B lender and still retains the client relationship for the future. This is a win-win for all parties. Due to the large volume of referrals to the partnering B lenders, clients usually get a lower rate and a better offer than if they went to a B lender on their own or through an independent broker.

CAN YOU FIT INTO THE BANKING BOX?

Let's discuss what the A lenders are looking for to get you approved. First and foremost, they want good credit. This is the foundation of all lending, and is the only way for banks to judge your creditworthiness for the future. If you always pay your bills on time and have never declared bankruptcy, chances are you will have good credit. But if you are the opposite, your credit bureau score will probably be too low for the banks to want to take the risk. Credit is ranked by an overall score given each person by the credit bureau agencies, usually Equifax or TransUnion. The scores range from as high as 900 to as low as 300. As a general guideline, the A lenders are looking for clients with scores above 680, and will automatically decline applications with scores under 600. Clients with scores in the low 520s to 600 are usually handled by B lenders at slightly higher rates to mitigate risk. Scores under 500 demonstrate very poor credit, and these clients will only be able to deal with C lenders. C lenders are a unique group, and sometimes seek private investors' funds if no lenders want to consider the file. These deals are always at the very highest rates, and could be for first, second, or third mortgage loans.

Watch out for smaller lenders, credit unions, or B and C lenders that might put stipulations on your mortgage. Most will offer a five-year loan with a lock-in for the first three years. This means that you will not be able to leave the lender or pay off your mortgage within the first three years. The only exception to this clause is if you were to sell your home and provide proof of the sale with a firm sale agreement.

If you have excellent credit with good, stable income, you will have no problem getting a mortgage or loan from any of the big banks. These lenders want good clients on their books, and compete with one another to offer the lowest rate. They will often pay you to switch your business, such as appraisal fees, discharge fees, title charges, and cash-backs to help pay for penalties with a competing lender. Put on your poker face and haggle with these lenders. You might be surprised at all the offers they make to get your business.

Here are some **major red flags** that banks look for.

1. SLOW PAYMENT ON CREDIT

When your credit bureau is pulled electronically by a lender, it will show how often and by how many days you have been late on your monthly payments. I cannot stress enough to clients the importance of good credit. It is your snapshot all lenders use to determine if you are a suitable risk.

Protect your credit, no matter how much you make. There are many high-income earners who are very sloppy with their credit, and get very upset when banks deny future credit or force the closure of credit cards and lines of credit.

In the coming years, good credit will become more important as all banks tighten their lending guidelines without offering any deviation for client situations. In the past, we used to be able to talk to lenders and persuade credit officers and adjudicators to take a chance on the client and be more lenient. No more. Nowadays, bad credit equals higher rates or lending restrictions to mitigate risk. Most people do not realize how important good credit is until they don't have it anymore. Don't abuse it. It will come back to bite you later, and you may be surprised at how big a bite it will take out of your future budget.

Be careful with cell phone companies. I have had countless clients' credit compromised by phone companies that post bad scores with credit bureaus because of disputes on their account. Refusing to pay your bill because of a dispute or error could do irreparable damage to your credit, and it is simply not worth it. Be mindful about keeping your credit clean, and do not try and skip out of a contract. You will never win. Once reported to the credit bureau, the damage is already done, and it is virtually impossible to remove it from your report. Don't let the phone company, or whatever credit company it might be, have that much power over your ability to get credit in the future. This is often referred to as a "merchant hand" controlling your future.

Below, I outline certain "R-ratings" that could be posted with your credit bureau and what to do to avoid them. Please keep in mind that once a rating is posted, regardless of whether it is corrected, paid off, or closed after the fact, the damage is already done. The R-rating will stay in the history section of your credit bureau for a period of four to six years before it drops off. Pretty scary. Be careful.

R1 Score: Marked on current delinquent accounts that have been inactive for more than 45 days but less than 90 days. These liabilities will move to an R9 status if not paid by the 90-day cutoff.

R8 Score: Notification of repossession; usually used by the automotive industry, and accompanied by vehicle identification numbers, as well as account and personal identification numbers.

R7 Score: This denotes a payment schedule plan, but is not often used anymore. Currently, Equifax and TransCanada Credit Union will post alerts to lenders when a credit bureau is requested. These are referred to in the industry as hawk alerts and raven scores that must be mitigated with an explanation and/or solution, provided in writing, with every lending application.

R9 Score: Delinquent revolving loan or credit facility that has been inactive for more than 90–120 days and has usually been written off by the lender and passed on to a collection agency. R9s demonstrate very poor creditworthiness, and whether it is your fault or not, having your loan go to collections forces a new lender to reconsider approval.

Once the loan has been written off, it is automatically posted to the credit bureau, and the delinquent liability will be given an R9 status until it is paid in full. Some clients believe that, if they explain their situation in writing or request the lender not to notify the credit bureau, they can avoid having messages posted to their credit report. Please believe me when I say this will never happen. Simply asking a creditor not to report to Equifax or TransCanada Credit Union is not possible, since this is an automatic process and government mandated.

2. TOO MUCH CREDIT

Over the last ten years, especially before the financial crisis of 2008, credit was very easy to acquire. Even now, with low interest rates, it is easy to qualify for more credit than is needed. I sometimes see clients with multiple credit cards, lines of credit, and store loans. Sometimes they don't even have balances on their cards, but want to know they have lots of credit available for their use.

For those of you who have many cards with zero balances, please know that the banks view this as a potential risk. They do not like clients to have multiple cards, even if your credit score is good. If you have a lot of open credit and ask the bank for a loan or mortgage, the lender will likely consider each credit card limit as maxed in order to mitigate risk. For example, even though you do not have a current balance on your Mastercard with a limit of $20,000, they will consider adding the maximum monthly payment to your ratios in the event you went out the next day and took a cash advance for the $20,000. Really, you only need two credit cards: a Mastercard, Visa, or American Express.

Don't fall into the trap of getting store cards to save 10% on your daily purchase. I have seen countless clients ruin their credit by consistently signing up for multiple store cards that they never use and become inactive.

I once had a client who had fifteen cards from one department store, all inactive. The A lender would not approve her request for credit, and she was forced to go to a B lender that charged her a much higher rate. Think twice before you sign up for that next card. Is it worth it?

3. NO CREDIT

If you had previous bad credit and now are just using cash, you are essentially handcuffing your future. Without re-establishing good credit, the banks will decline you every time.

If you are new to the country or just starting out, it is best to start acquiring credit slowly. There are countless new immigrant programs available to newcomers, and most banks have different methods to determine your creditworthiness when applying for loans. As a newcomer, it is best to establish a relationship with one of the big banks. Most banks give special favouritism to their own clients because they have a history with them. The lending practices with all lenders are definitely more stringent with new clients versus existing clients who have a good banking history.

4. PROPERTY TAXES IN ARREARS

If you have been in arrears on your property taxes for a long time and it is reported to your credit bureau, this is a huge red flag for the banks. The A lenders will issue an automatic decline. The reason for this is that municipal governments always have precedence over the banks, and if you have not paid your property taxes, the banks assume you will probably be delinquent on a mortgage loan also. Banks are not in the habit of foreclosing on clients. They will certainly move forward with legal action if necessary, but it is bad for business, and therefore all A lenders have made it a standard practice across the board not to lend to any client with property taxes in arrears. They would prefer to avoid the situation from the beginning, rather than entering into what could be a potential future problem. To ensure this does not happen, most lenders will add the property tax portion to your monthly mortgage payment and pay the municipality or county on your behalf.

5. SUPPORT PAYMENTS IN ARREARS

If you have been delinquent in paying child or alimony support and it is reported to your credit bureau, A lenders will automatically decline your request for credit. Regardless of the reason, it demonstrates to the banks a lack of creditworthiness.

I have seen many times over the past twenty years where clients have valid reasons for either being late or refusing to pay support. Usually, it is because there is some type of unresolved dispute the client feels strongly about. Please remember that the banks really don't care. They are in the business of lending millions of dollars out to people every day, and if in the past you have demonstrated delinquency in resolving credit issues, the banks will not take the risk. You will be penalized by having to get a higher interest rate loan from a B or C lender to mitigate risk. Be careful and mindful of your commitments.

6. BANKRUPTCY

Declaring bankruptcy is a last resort for most, and the credit situation is usually dire. Yes, the bankruptcy will ruin your credit; however, it is recoverable. Once the bankruptcy has been settled and cleared, it is important to re-establish good credit right away. Usually, clients will have to get a pre-paid Visa or Mastercard to get started. If you do not re-establish good credit, it will become increasingly difficult to get back into the lower rates offered by the A lenders.

If the A lenders see good re-established credit over two or three years from your bankruptcy discharge, they will lend. Often, such clients are fearful of credit and tend to use cash for everything after the bankruptcy, and then are very surprised that banks decline them. Even if your bankruptcy was ten years ago, but you have never re-established any new credit, the banks will automatically decline.

7. INCOME TAXES IN ARREARS

Banks usually discover if you are in arrears on your income taxes when they ask to see your tax return. We are also finding more and more A lenders now requesting to see your last year's Notice of Assessment. This used to be a mandatory requirement of self-employed clients or contractors, but it is now becoming required of more lenders to confirm that a new client is up to date on their personal taxes. If you have a high credit score above 680 and have regular employment income, most A lenders will want only a current paystub and your prior year's W-2 or T-4 slip.

Only if your credit scores are low will banks dig a little deeper to ensure you are a suitable risk. It is a good idea to pay off any unpaid income taxes before you apply for credit with the banks, and make sure to keep proof of payment. Often the bank will lend to clients on the stipulation that taxes be paid either before the loan is advanced or from the proceeds of the proposed loan.

If you are self-employed and write off all your income with expenses to avoid paying income tax, good luck getting a loan from a bank. You can't have it both ways! By showing a very low income on your tax return and Notice of Assessment, you are completely eliminating your ability to borrow. The banks will use only your net income when qualifying you for a loan.

I once had a client who made over $200,000, which he reported as business income on his tax return; however, he paid income tax only on $1,100 because he wrote off all his income with business expenses. This was great for the client, who paid little to no personal income tax, but when it came to qualifying for a mortgage with a bank, he was declined. Even when we tried a special stated-income program with an alternative B lender, the client was still declined.

8. CURRENT MORTGAGE IN ARREARS

It goes without saying that, if your current mortgage is in arrears, it will be virtually impossible for a new lender to mitigate the potential risk of giving you a new mortgage. It always surprises me when clients fail to understand why they are being turned down for a loan or mortgage when they are behind on their payments. Think about it: if you planned to lend

$200,000 of your own money to your neighbour who had a history of never paying on time or who had other loans with you that he never paid off, would you give him more money? Probably not.

People think that they can deceive the lenders and perhaps if they don't say anything, the bank won't find out that they are behind on their payments. Well, this doesn't happen anymore. As of 2012, all lenders in Canada and most in the United States have begun to share information across all lending platforms. Once your credit bureau file is electronically pulled using your Social Insurance Number, it instantly becomes apparent what you have in credit, along with a full history of your past repayment habits and job history. Be careful. Gone are the days of sweeping it under the rug and borrowing more to get creditors off your back. Today, clients will discover a totally different lending landscape—one that is tougher and requires clients to be accountable for their past indiscretions. The use of new mandated government guidelines continues to force banks to tighten lending requirements. We have seen this government involvement year-over-year, so be careful to keep your credit clean.

WAYS TO SAVE EVERY DAY

CONSIDER THE VALUES CONTINUALLY DEMONSTRATED IN THE BUSINESS world when reviewing your own finances. Companies big and small regularly cut costs and review fiscal spending every year. They have a responsibility to their shareholders and their employees to ensure the business is continuously profitable. If it is not, they look for ways to trim spending and increase cash flow. If businesses spend too much or try to expand too fast, they run the risk of going into bankruptcy. You, as the CEO of your finances, also have the responsibility of reviewing your expenditures annually.

There are many ways that you can save every day. Simply by being more conscious of how much you are spending and where the funds are going, you will develop ways to save, postpone, or perhaps eliminate the constant drain on your money. Here are some simple tips to help you get started. Look for your own personal ways to save. Make it a personal challenge to the new, wealthier you.

HOME

Cut out the house cleaning and lawn care services.

Do your own gardening and lawn maintenance. You can save a bundle by fertilizing your own lawn, rather than paying for this service.

When doing home improvement that requires expensive tools, rent them instead of buying.

Do small repairs and improvements yourself, rather than automatically hiring a service. You will be surprised at what you can do, and will feel empowered by your accomplishments. Check the internet for tips.

Cut down on your phone services. Consider eliminating your land line at home if you use your cell phone all the time.

Cut down on your cable service. Beware of all the upgrades and bundle services that soon add up to a hefty monthly charge.

Bundle insurance policies to get lower annual rates. When you have your home, auto, and life insurance with the same company, you will get significant reductions in premiums.

Check the classified ads. There are always things for sale. It is a great way to furnish your home or basement.

Reuse your stuff. Find new uses for things that you want to replace. Paint it, change it. What could you use it for now?

Stop buying. Value your items. It was cherished when you first bought it; why did you lose interest?

Adopt a more vintage, eclectic lifestyle.

Choose Energy Star–rated appliances when you have to purchase new ones.

Get a programmable thermostat so that you can turn the furnace down during the day when you are out of the house or at work.

AUTOMOTIVE

Drive your car longer. Repair your car when needed, instead of trading it in just because of high mileage.

Never lease your car. Most choose to lease their vehicles for tax purposes, especially if they are self-employed; however, you can still write off your vehicle by annual depreciation. Talk to your accountant.

Car pool to work or take public transit. It's a great way to increase the lifespan of your car, to socialize with friends, rest, or read a good book.

Do your own oil changes. My husband has been doing his own oil changes for the past fifteen years, and it must be a "macho man" thing, because he brags about it to all his male friends.

Get tire insurance when you buy new tires. In the past I would have discouraged getting it, but the new tire insurance is usually quite cheap. We bought it for $7.00 a tire at a national tire retailer, and within six months we ran over a nail and needed a new tire because it could not be repaired. The retailer replaced it for free. That was a great savings.

PERSONAL

Keep membership and club fees to a minimum. Try to limit the amount of extracurricular activities and annual fees.

Buy generic brands when you can.

Use coupons. Check through your newspaper flyers and find sales.

Buy in bulk. Become a member of a "big box" store such as Costco. Better yet, go with a member to avoid paying the annual fee and to buy in bulk.

Buy at discount stores and outlets. Shop when there are sales.

Get retailers to price match. Most retailers are now advertising this feature to encourage shoppers to do all their shopping at one place.

Don't pay a higher price for things just because the store is nicer inside. Beware the ambiance and shopping mood that stores work so hard to create. Don't get enticed to pay more for items just because you are romanced by the surroundings and staff. Remember, this shopping sensation is designed to get you to part with your hard-earned money, not to help you get to retirement.

Sell your old clothing to consignment stores. There are many new high-end consignment stores that will buy your designer clothes, shoes, boots, and handbags. Don't forget, this is a great place to shop for your wardrobe, too.

Use points programs that retailers offer, and shop at stores that give points and discount specials.

Buy clothing at the end of the season when it is always marked down. Buy household items, sports, and outdoor equipment also at the end of the season when there is less demand and retailers are trying to make room for new stock.

Use dry cleaners infrequently. Iron and press your own clothes. Buy a steamer or fabric press and try hand washing your delicate clothing. Why not hang your suit or clothes outside for the day? Hanging your clothes outdoors instantly removes odours, forces the wrinkles to fall out, and is nature's organic and chemical-free version of today's dry cleaning.

Don't buy organic foods. Have a garden, and learn to freeze and can your fruits and vegetables. Go to "pick-your-own" farms—it's a great outing and cheap fun.

Buy used books, DVDs, and CDs. Visit thrift stores or local auctions. You will be amazed at the great deals.

Consider warranty insurance on products only if it is cheap or you think you might use it in the near future.

Go to garage sales, farmers' markets, and auctions. Someone's junk could be your treasure. Don't forget to sell your things this way, too. The power of the internet is also at your fingertips. It is so easy to sell and buy things today.

Consider buying everything used, and keep your things longer. Resist the desire to upsize and upgrade.

Ask for discounts when you buy. Don't be afraid to ask for a 10% discount if the item you want to purchase is a little damaged. Often, retailers will give you a discount if you ask.

Cut out the pet groomers. Cut your pet's hair and nails yourself. Buying the right grooming tools is a one-time investment in future savings. The pets don't need the costs—they just want your attention, and that's free.

It feels good to get a deal! Have that feeling more often. Look for opportunities to save, and take advantage of sales and promotional offers. Become addicted to saving!

PERSONAL BANKING

Never pay annual fees for credit cards. Keep the number of cards to a minimum (having only two credit cards should be your goal).

Get rid of your line of credit. Having available credit is an invitation to go into debt. Avoid it as much as possible. If you must have a credit line, ensure it is secured to lower the rate of interest. Having an unsecured line of credit at a much higher interest rate only makes money for the banks and invites opportunities for you to go back into debt. Be careful.

Make your children pay for half or all of their college or university education. This is a good way to instil financial responsibility in young adults. Teaching them to work part time and save will ensure that they are more able to handle money in the future. You might even find that they work harder at their studies because they don't want to pay to repeat a low-grade course. They now have a vested interest in their future success.

Limit your bank fees. Look for banks that will offer discounts or free banking if you have other products with them, such as a credit card, TFSA, or your mortgage.

Don't get overdraft on your bank account. You do not need it if you are using your Trackers. It is a terrible habit that some people get into and can never get out of. Most banks charge 21% interest on funds used from overdraft. It is never worth it.

Never continuously refinance your mortgage to consolidate debts.

WHEN SELLING OR BUYING A HOME, CONSIDER THESE SAVINGS TIPS

Keep bridge loans short. These are the bank loans that bridge the funds when your purchase and your sale do not match up with the same closing date. Often, it is great to have two or three days in-between your closings so that you don't have to move into your new home in a hurried rush. Remember that bridge loans are demand loans with no option for insurance. If something happens during a long bridge, you could be on the hook for thousands of dollars. Also, bridge loans are not cheap. The banks charge high interest on these loans, so it is better to keep them only a few days, not many weeks.

Move yourself. Even though it is easier with movers, they are expensive. Instead, rustle up your muscular friends and make it a moving party. The money you save could go toward having the furnace and ducts cleaned or something else that requires a professional service.

Don't pay for home rental services, such as water heaters. When you buy, get the vendor to pay out the contract before you take occupancy. These contracts are an unnecessary monthly expense.

Shop for the best mortgage rates, and make sure your bank pays any costs or penalties if they are keeping your business. Never extend your amortization to longer than twenty years. Avoid amortizations of twenty-five or thirty years, no matter what your banker says. The added interest takes up too much of your monthly payment and is not worth it in the long run.

ENTERTAINMENT AND OUTINGS

Never buy a vacation on credit unless you are using it for the points and then paying it off immediately.

Consider family camping trips over expensive all-inclusive resort vacations. Young children love these vacations.

Go on "mini-breaks" of only a few days or over a long weekend. Avoid expensive vacations unless you have saved up the funds.

Sign up for magazine subscriptions instead of buying off the rack. Often, you can order magazine subscriptions through points programs.

Take lunches to school and work.

Stop the takeout and restaurant meals. There is nothing better than a home-cooked meal. Restaurant meals are high in calories and should be restricted for special occasions only.

Cut down on the cost of purchasing multiple coffees a day, especially the expensive lattes and cappuccinos. Consider getting a coffee machine at your desk and treat yourself to some specialty blend coffees.

With the exception of safety helmets, consider buying used sports equipment. Find stores that buy and sell gently used sports equipment.

Eliminate your gym membership and walk or jog for free around your neighbourhood. Replace your personal trainer with workout books and DVDs. They say that jogging is the "poor man's liposuction," so get out there and start pounding the pavement instead of paying for plastic surgery.

Go to the movies on "Cheap Night," and use the points and discount cards to get future savings. Most movie chains will have a discount movie day once a week/month.

Collect your points and then order items to give as gifts for Christmas and birthdays. The gifts are free, but the recipient doesn't have to know.

INVESTING 101:

The Basics

THERE ARE LOTS OF BOOKS ON HOW TO INVEST AND PLAY THE STOCK market, and I am not going to delve too much into the intricacies of the market. Suffice it to say that you need to create a portfolio that you can live with during up-markets and downturns. You should never live or die by your portfolio, and if you are in this situation, you need to get into something less risky. Let's take a little "risk test."

Say you have $10,000 in cash and we are sitting at a table together. Your $10,000—in all its hundred-dollar-bill glory—is put in a nice big pile in the middle of the table. Okay, now let's play the market. I have a quarter: "heads," you get to keep your money; "tails," you lose it. Okay, I know this is an extreme example, but sometimes that's how it feels when you are watching your investments.

Let's try again. If you lost 20% of your investment portfolio, would you be okay with that? Yes? What if your portfolio was $1,000,000. A 20% loss is $200,000. Are you still comfortable with this possibility?

Most people say they can handle the ups and downs of the market, but research shows that we tend to hold on to losing positions far too long in the hope of avoiding errors or suffering a loss. We like to think that we are rational in our decisions, but most evidence suggests that investors act irrationally and have frequent errors in judgment. Some of us will even take a hands-off approach to stock picks, and hold on to securities that are familiar or ones to which we have an emotional attachment.

When I was an advisor for a large investment firm and wanted to sell out a declining stock position, my manager advised me not to. He said, "Why close the barn door when the horse has bolted? You need to leave it open for when the horse comes back." Well, the horse and the stock price never came back. The stock continued to go down and stayed down for over a year. Now what?

If you think you can predict the outcome of a stock, wake up. The reality is that you cannot. Becoming overconfident creates unwarranted faith in your stock pick, which is often made without all the immense flow of information that is *not* available to the average investor. Clients will make an educated guess without understanding potential underlying dangers. By the time you get the information on a stock, it is already old news to the market makers. Always assume that the seller knows more than the buyer.

Ask yourself these questions: What is your breaking point? If we had another financial crisis like 2008, how would you feel? In 2008, investment advisors told their clients that they were well diversified in a variety of secure sectors; however, all sectors went down. Today, after we feel things have normalized in the market, we now know a buy-and-hold philosophy no longer works due to increased volatility and continuous worldwide market changes.

Not everyone acts the same with loss, and it is best to have your portfolio managed by a licensed investment advisor and firm you trust. Make sure you understand the products you are choosing with your advisor, and always invest to the point that you can sleep at night. It is so important for you to create your own competitive advantage and to choose investment products that match your future goals and risk tolerance. Don't worry so much about the gossiping and bad news stories. You cannot be a profit-chasing gambler, and if it sounds too good to be true, you know it probably is.

In 2009, the stock market went down more than 50%, and there was no guarantee that this was the bottom. There seemed to be no compelling reason to invest. Since then, the Canadian stock market has recovered 100% and the US stock market has increased 200%. Markets right now are at fair value or slightly below fair value. Talk to your investment advisor and get good advice to select for the coming decade. Take a look at the bigger picture, and decide with your advisor if now is the time to take advantage of good opportunities. Remember, the secret to wealth is not to own anything that eats while you sleep. This means don't choose investments that eat away at your hard-earned capital in the hope of hitting a big score. If the risk is too large, it is not something for which you should risk your CORE.

Here are the two most common investment styles you may wish to explore. Both can be very good at producing your desired results, and it is imperative that you get the right investment advisor for each style. As your investment portfolio grows over time, you should always re-evaluate your products and style of investing. Here we will discuss the basics of each.

FIXED INCOME INVESTING

Fixed income investing is primarily a rules-based investment philosophy that takes all emotion out of the equation. You simply follow the rules and get a solid return. Laddering is the most common method used with bonds, and today $11 trillion is invested in this method. Even with all the problems since the financial crisis of 2008, fixed income managers still have not gone into the securities sector because of lower yields. When analyzing the markets from a long-term perspective, the fixed income portfolios win every time through laddered techniques. Almost all large corporate and government pension funds are done through this method to provide stability and security to the overall investment portfolio. In a true laddered portfolio, you don't care about the changes in the yield curve based on current interest rates. Every year, you simply reinvest the maturing funds. This is a long-term investment strategy that could be set up to match certain stages of your life.

Fixed income products consist mostly of different types of bonds, and buying bonds is much like buying real estate. You can't turn around and sell them immediately after the purchase for a profit, as you can with stocks. It is a guaranteed product that over time will have a higher value than your purchase price, typically without the loss of your initial investment. Most people who invest in real estate and want a tangible asset choose to diversify their investments in institutional bonds because of the similarities.

All stock picks, mutual funds, and exchange-traded funds are based on past performance and technical analysis, but how do you know if you are buying in at the right time? You might be purchasing at the top market value, only to be unhappy when you see the price of your mutual fund pull back. Most people find it difficult to commit to regular contributions if there is no guarantee of return due to stock risk. With bonds you have a finite return. You know what you invested, what the duration is, and what you are getting back at redemption. There is no guessing. You simply cash out your profit at the end of the term.

Not all bonds are the same. There is a vast array of bonds to choose from, and it is best to have your advisor discuss all the different features and benefits. I have always favoured institutional compounding strip bonds, which are great for a Canadian RRSP portfolio since the gains are not taxable while in the plan. The longer-term bonds actually have a greater simple interest rate than other fixed income products. Most bonds simply run the term and pay out at the end, whereas compounding bonds roll in the annual returns, adding them to your principal amount and then begin compounding again. On their own, these annual return amounts are too insignificant, but when they are compounded in the bond, it is almost magical. It works every time, consistently, without risk, providing the returned profit to your portfolio.

You could set up a laddered portfolio to match debt loads that you wish to pay off with the proceeds at maturity. Laddering your bonds into bite-sized chunks also gives you diversity to provide for any anticipated purchases or future commitments. If you choose bonds for all or part of your portfolio, make sure this is a transactional-based portfolio with a promise of a minimum floor rate and duration. Together with your advisor, be sure to pick the best institutional triple-A bonds that offer your anticipated compounded return with security.

GUIDED STOCK PORTFOLIOS

This is the method of choice when thinking of investing for the future. Most people will partner with a financial planner or investment advisor to put their money into the stock market. Today, more than ever, we have found a massive expertise gap in stock picking, and most advisors will cling to guided portfolios, mutual funds, and managed funds. We have moved from the old stock broker style to a managed concept with annual fees. These programs are designed to protect the advisor and brokerage firms and to limit potential damage to a client's portfolio. Advisors will often say that clients are too emotional and reactive about their stock portfolio and should consider buying opportunities when the stock prices fall. This is true. Just don't take things at face value. Make sure you do your homework.

Just like sales at retail stores, when customers see 50%-off signs in store windows, they flock to get in on the good deals. This doesn't happen in the stock market, but it should. Let's look at an example. Royal Bank stock, typically sitting at around $50–58 took a nose dive in the fall of 2013 down to $33. People were in a panic, and stories were floating everywhere with widespread speculation that it would go down even further. In the spring of 2014, the stock price was over $70 and continued to go up for the balance of the year. It is best to speak to your advisor about future opportunities and make sure you don't have your portfolio sitting on autopilot. It is also advantageous to purchase stock through an automatic monthly purchase program so that you can take advantage of dips in the market and the concept of dollar-cost-averaging.

Just giving your advisor $300,000 and saying, "Okay, I want a 15% return," won't work. No one will ever guarantee a return in a stock or mutual fund portfolio. This is a far different world than the guarantees of a fixed income strategy. All clients are focused on the health of their financial lifestyle and want little to no uncertainty, so diversification is the key to ensuring long-term stability in your stock portfolio.

Big account holders should always deal with a top-tier firm because of all the value-added services they provide. The large, bank-run firms are licensed investment dealers, which are heavily regulated and governed by strict rules of conduct and practices by governments and other self-regulatory organizations. You wouldn't think of buying your groceries at a convenience store, so why invest in a small, unregulated investment firm?

Large firms will showcase their sophistication in wealth management, financial and estate planning, trusts, business planning, and business successions. These firms will also have proprietary programs that follow specific methodologies for picking and choosing different stocks such as managed programs with annual fees. Your advisor might choose to use some of these product selections along with the advisor's own picks to further customize your portfolio.

TIP: **Your financial objective should always be focused on how to secure capital with adequate growth in the most tax-efficient manner, including debt management.**

Many people look for a better way to manage the complexity and choice that comes with personal investing, and they think it has to be complicated to justify a large return. It really does not. By choosing a fixed income/bond portfolio, guided stock portfolio, or a combination of the two, you can create your own self-actualized investment program. Be involved in your investment decisions with your advisor. Create the portfolio you are most comfortable with so that you can do what you want in retirement and feel confident with the choices you have made to create your financial security. Rather than just filling time in retirement, you can set things up now, so that you can live out your dreams in the future.

Here are some key focus points to discuss with your advisor:

- products for the protection of lifestyle;
- understanding your vision of retirement and your personal risk tolerance;
- accumulation strategies versus just focusing on money management and managed portfolios;
- understand the fee structures, embedded costs, and management or trailer fees;
- Explore different products that generate consistent, stable returns regardless of day-to-day market activity.

HUMAN CAPITAL

If now is not the time to invest because you are in the early stages of wealth building, don't underestimate your ability to still make money. It is said that the fastest way to create more wealth is to believe in your ability to earn more. Consider the thought of buying stock in yourself. Investing in yourself, going back to school and learning something new can increase your income immensely. Your most important asset is your ability to make more money. Believe that you are worth more, and break free to declare your independence.

RETIREMENT DREAMING:

Debt-Free with a Comfortable Retirement Future

YOU'RE DRIVING IN YOUR CAR TO WORK AND YOU'RE LATE. YOU COME to the top of a hill and can see in the distance a sea of cars lined up. They are all funnelling into a single laneway that leads to the road you must go on. So what do you do? Do you get in line at the end and wait patiently with all the other cars? Or do you speed on past the dozens of cars lined up, look for an opening in the line, and then slam on your brakes and squeeze in, bypassing all the cars you would have had to wait behind?

Depending on where you are in life, chances are you are going to have to do the latter. If you are just starting out, you have lots of time to invest and save over many years, taking 10% from your paycheque toward a retirement fund. Most of us have been mired down with kids, careers, homes, cars, and big debt, so we are going to have to skip lining up in the slow lane and make the right choices for our retirement. This means we may have to skip ahead a little and be more aggressive about our future planning.

Now, I am not saying that you need to run out and get the most aggressive stock portfolio you can find—far from it. However, those who are a little more aggressive and open-minded will have a higher return than those who are completely afraid of any risk at all. Most people are generally risk averse, but we also have debt. We like our comforts, want to retire sooner and with enough money to continue our lifestyle. To do that, you have to have a plan. Try to consider alternative investments such as rental properties, laddered portfolios, and tax-efficient savings products. Always ensure the investments you choose have an acceptable risk to your capital and have the added benefit of compounded growth year over year. Simply relying on guaranteed investment certificates with a return of 1–2% is not going to help you reach the savings you will need.

Be sure to have your CORE finances set up first, and work at paying off your retail debt. It is fine to have a mortgage, but make sure you don't have any other debt. Keep your budget tight, and make sure you are looking at the bigger picture. Keep your mortgage amortization locked on your retirement age, so that you retire with no debt. And above all, avoid the "refi-habit."

PREPARE FOR THE "HONEYMOON STAGE": JOHN AND MARIA

When the phone rang and I realized it was John, I was so pleased to hear from him. John and Maria had been clients of mine many years ago when I refinanced their mortgage to consolidate debt. I hadn't spoken to them in about ten years, so we spent some time chatting about life, kids, new grandchildren, and their home of thirty years. John was now retired from the school board with a small pension for his twenty-seven years as a custodian. Maria had worked for the same service company as a receptionist for thirty-one years, and retired the previous year with no pension. I was surprised to hear they still had a mortgage, now much larger than the one we did together many years ago. They had refinanced their mortgage many times over the past thirty years, and now wanted to do it again in retirement. Their mortgage was $257,000, and they had recently purchased a truck on their line of credit for $53,500. They were finding it hard to make the payments now that their incomes had changed. They wanted to consolidate the truck loan into a new mortgage with a longer amortization to make the payments lower and easier month to month. John had already been to his bank, which turned him down. He didn't understand why.

American and Canadian banks are not as freewheeling as they used to be years ago. Since the financial crisis of 2008, we have seen a steady increase in credit tightening. The federal government has passed many new lending guidelines, and the banks now are very cautious about advancing more credit. It is predicted that the policies and procedures for lending will only get tighter over the years as we find more people turning to credit to supplement their lifestyle.

The reason the bank turned down John and Maria was *not* that they were asking for more money, but that they were asking to pay less by extending the amortization on a new mortgage. The bank viewed this as a risk that, under current guidelines, could not mitigate the twenty-five-year period it would take to pay it off, since John was already sixty-eight. Of course, there will always be a lender who would do this deal, but at a higher rate. With the rate now higher, it would negate the whole reason for doing the refinance.

John and Maria are stuck. They can no longer do what they have always done: refinance to make it easier. Because of their age and fixed retirement income, the door to refinancing was now closed. They must make their payments and pay for what they owe. With little to no savings and investments, this is a harsh reality that you do not want to face once retired. These clients will need to sell their home, pay off their debts, and move to an apartment to live on the house proceeds from the sale. Please don't let this happen. Make a plan now, and ensure you take care of yourself for the future. If you don't do it, no one else will.

So, now that you're thinking about retirement, let's take some time to talk about where you are today and where you want to be in the next five, ten, or twenty years. Answer the following questions, and be honest with yourself.

- How comfortable do you feel financially?
- How do you spend your money today?
- How do you plan to spend in the future?
- Will you spend more or less when in retirement?
- What kinds of activities are you planning to do after working?
- Do you plan to work part time in retirement? For how many years?

One out of every two North Americans will live to ninety-two, and one out of every four will live to over ninety-five. With fewer people having pension plans, it is imperative that you start your own defined-benefit plan through an investment portfolio, with rental or investment properties, or by using a fixed income ladder.

Over 40% of Americans and Canadians underestimate their spending in retirement and when surveyed, 90% of retirees were not able to cut back on their spending as planned once in retirement. The harsh reality is that they were not able to lower their standard of living drastically once they stopped working, and found that, in the first few years, there seemed to be a very high burn rate. When people first retire, they often have a high degree of pent-up demand for certain unanticipated expenditures. How can you blame them? Most new retirees are healthy and active, and all those pictures they have been cutting out of the travel section of the paper for the past couple of years look like great places to visit. This is called the "Honeymoon Stage."

THE BUCKET APPROACH TO RETIREMENT SAVINGS

Your personal plan must be able to provide easily for your retirement goals, and the best way is to follow what is called the Bucket Approach. You might already have close to the recommended savings guidelines for each segment, but are still grappling with retail and mortgage debt that you will need to eliminate. Conversely, you could have your debt and mortgage paid off, and are just starting to think about your long-term savings. Whatever the case may be, use the Bucket Approach as a framework that you can easily adjust based on your income, ability to save, and your plans for the future.

In the following example, we have divided your savings goals into three categories, or buckets, with recommended savings targets for each. This division of future savings ensures you will be ready for each phase of your retirement journey.

BUCKET ONE: HONEYMOON PHASE, YEARS 1–5 OF RETIREMENT
Estimated: $100,000–200,000 in unregistered savings plan or TFSAs + part-time incomes (optional).

BUCKET TWO: RETIREMENT SAVINGS, YEARS 6–20 OF RETIREMENT
Estimated: $300,000–500,000 mixed investments, RRSPs + pensions + CPP/OAS + rental income (optional).

BUCKET THREE: LONG-TERM PENSION, YEARS 20+ OF RETIREMENT

Estimated: $200,000–400,000 laddered institutional compounding bonds, fixed income LIP (laddered investment portfolio), RRSPs or RIFs. **This bucket could be reduced or eliminated with proceeds from the sale of your primary residence if downsizing.*

Let's look a little closer at each phase.

In **Bucket One, the Honeymoon Phase ($100,000–$200,000 saved)**, you will be able to use these funds freely for the early part of your retirement. It is a good idea to have your savings in a tax-free savings plan or an unregistered savings plan so that you can use these funds freely without any tax hit. With a monthly pension or income from a part-time job, it will be easy for you to live without touching the funds in Bucket Two. Bucket Two will continue to grow tax free in a registered investment.

In **Bucket Two (minimum $300,000)**, you will need to consider the income stream that should last you through years six to twenty of your retirement. If you do not have a pension plan, you will need to ensure that these funds are closer to the $500,000 mark. By pensionizing your portfolio into fixed income investments, you will be able to ensure that your capital is preserved and your growth will be compounding yearly.

Bucket Three (minimum $200,000) will give you long-term security and ensure that any added costs of homecare or health-related expenditures can be easily maintained. By being financially stable, you will ensure your quiet comfort in old age without having to make sacrifices because of declining health or necessary long-term care. This bucket can be reduced or eliminated if you plan to sell your home to downsize and use the proceeds to fund this phase.

The Bucket Approach is a simple and an easy concept that you can tweak and customize to your anticipated lifestyle. Remember, money in retirement is the by-product of a well-thought-out and successful plan. If you do not have any debt when retiring, you will be able to live in your home with minimal expenses. Start planning for that someday now. I can promise that this process will work.

LET'S TALK ABOUT RRSPS

Registered Retirement Savings Plans are a fabulous way to help you save for your future, ensuring your invested funds grow tax free until the withdrawal. Nowadays most people agree that we cannot base our retirement future on government pension allowances. Trying to live on a small government-subsidized pension income would be virtually impossible for most Canadians with debt. This is why planning and saving early is so important, and RRSPs should be an integral part of your investment portfolio.

When asked how much you will really need at retirement, most advisors suggest planning to have 60% of your final year's earnings with no outstanding debt encumbrances on your monthly taxable income. That being said, today's retirees are different than they were years ago. They are healthier and living longer, working longer, and pursuing goals that previous generations never would have considered. Today's markets are also very different, highly manipulated by the global economy, extremely volatile, and definitely not a "buy and hold" marketplace. If RRSPs are your only method of saving for the future, then I say start early and always put the maximum allowable amount in every year. There is always a place for RRSPs in your portfolio, and there is a mountain of information out there about how to define your contributions. Invest with a professional, and try not to cash in your registered investments until you really are retired so that you avoid paying high income taxes.

Debt reduction should always be your number one priority. Invest in RRSPs every year and be open to diversifying your portfolio with other investments. Remember not to have all your eggs in one basket. Asset diversification has always been the number one secret of the ultra-rich.

Consider building your own financial team. You should not do this alone. Today, information abounds, and there are so many professionals in the investment and retirement field who can help you. Consider financial planners or investment advisors, insurance agents, accountants, or a personal finance coach. Do your homework. This is your hard-earned money we are talking about, and you don't want to take undue risks. I have seen portfolios decimated by well-meaning investment advisors in the past. It is important for you to get advice and then double check it.

Interview your new financial teammates and make sure they are on board with your plan to help you get where you need to go—to reach your dreams in retirement, not their monthly quota. Don't do it alone. Remember to be the CEO of your finances. As the owner of your financial future, you will need to rely on experts, but do your homework, and make sure they are the right fit for you and your plan.

Ask for what you want; it is the best way to ensure you will get it. Ultimately, you must have control, and if your banker isn't concerned about getting you debt-free and wealthier, find another. Remember, you will be the only one to blame if you don't have enough at retirement.

Retiring with money is expected of you. Have faith in yourself. It's okay to be discouraged—it won't happen overnight. Remember, no one has a challenge-free life, but you will want to minimize those challenges in your retirement. Chances are you will not be able to recover from major monetary challenges when in retirement, and you won't want to resort to drastic decisions and sacrifices. Where you are in retirement is based on what you do over the next few years until you get there. You can retire comfortably without debt, and you owe it to yourself to try. Here are some more questions to ponder while you are making your own personal plan.

- How long do you have until retirement? Create a personal timeline.
- What does a "comfortable retirement" mean to you? Be specific and make a list.
- What is most important to you?
- What aspects of your life have the highest priority?
- What is your current financial situation?
- What plans have you made to maintain your family's lifestyle?
- Are you prepared for emergencies?
- Do you anticipate having debt in retirement?
- How do you plan to fund your retirement?
- Have you thought about long-term care and discussed options with your family?
- How current is your Will? Do you have a Living Will? Do you have a Power of Attorney?
- Do you have a work pension? Have you reviewed the plan?
- What investments do you have and what are your plans for acquiring more?
- How have you protected your assets? Do you have life and/or disability insurance?

PROTECTION OF LIFESTYLE

IF YOU WERE IN A CAR ACCIDENT TOMORROW AND DIED, WOULD YOUR family be okay financially? Most Americans and Canadians would say yes. People know that they must have insurance to cover one-time costs on their demise, such as the funeral, taxes, and mortgages. They also usually plan for expenses that will continue after their death to provide for their spouse and children. When we give clients advice about protecting their future, we always reference our acronym WILT, which stands for Wills, Income Protection, Life Insurance, and Tax Planning. You will always need an up-to-date Will to ensure your estate is divided the way you wish and all minor children are taken care of. Income protection is often overlooked and considered too costly by those who feel they have sufficient disability insurance with their employer. Most people concentrate on life insurance, but it is important to remember that most accidents do not result in death; you are more apt to be badly hurt or disabled and unable to continue working. Taxing planning is our last asset protection tip and is essential for building wealth. Insurance is a great tool to pay for capital gains tax that your estate will owe upon your death; if you are a business owner, it provides benefits that are protected against creditors.

DR. CARREL

Dr. John Carrel was a very successful chiropractor and a client of mine for many years. Ten years ago he took out a guaranteed renewable disability income policy that gave him income protection for his practice. He always complained about the payments, but knew that he had to protect his business income since he was the family's primary breadwinner. He had four girls and a wife who did not work. Dr. Carrel had a big Honda Goldwing motorbike that he rode in the summer, and decided to join a friend in taking a motorcycle driving course at a local college. The friend was a new driver and not yet licensed. The course apparently had something for all, promising to provide new driving techniques for already-licensed drivers like Dr. Carrel. So, the two of them went to the course; however, they were not allowed to use their own motorbikes. The school provided learning bikes, and Dr. Carrel was given a dirt bike. Well, let's just say that didn't work out well. Dr. Carrel flipped the bike and was badly hurt. He broke four fingers on his right hand and shattered his elbow, ulna, and wrist. With no use of his right hand or arm, Dr. Carrel was forced into retirement at age forty-nine, and thanks to his disability insurance could expect a tax-exempted monthly income of $21,300 until he turned sixty-five. Insurance can be costly, and most people will make excuses to avoid paying the premiums. But don't be so quick to decline it, because you never know when you will really need it. Part of your CORE plan must be to protect your assets. That includes you!

Protection of lifestyle can also include an understanding of your vision of retirement and the ways to provide a means to an end. There are many ways that you can use insurance policies not only to provide the necessary death benefit, but also as an accumulation strategy that makes good sense for your future wealth building. Besides the obvious benefits, there are policies that can act as saving tools that you can cash out if needed at retirement. It is best to speak to a licensed insurance agent, who will discuss your needs and be able to customize policies and products for you and your family. Here, I'll touch on the basics of what is available today for life insurance.

TERM INSURANCE

Term insurance is an insurance policy for a guaranteed amount and a set term. It is the cheapest of all insurance policies, and is only valid for the term you choose. So, if you take out a term of ten years and do not renew it, then die in the eleventh year, you receive nothing. There are three types of term policies:

1. Level term: no increase in premiums.
2. Increasing term: premiums increase over time.
3. Decreasing term: premiums remain the same on a decreasing policy per year.

BEST CHOICE: A RENEWABLE AND CONVERTIBLE TERM POLICY

Most people purchase a term policy because this is the least expensive type. A term policy can provide security for a specific period, during which an unexpected tragedy could result in the most catastrophic damage to your family's lifestyle. Consider getting a term policy that is renewable and/or convertible so that, when you are reaching the end of your term, you have the choice to continue the policy without having to go through the qualification process again.

Renewable means that you can automatically renew your policy without evidence of insurability, such as having to take a medical exam.

Convertible means that you can convert it to a permanent life policy without any evidence of insurability, without an incontestability period, and without a suicide clause. For example, if you were diagnosed with cancer, you could convert to a whole life policy and be automatically approved.

T-100 INSURANCE

This is the cheapest and most basic version of the whole life policy products. The product offers no cash value or dividends, and you continue to pay the premiums until you reach one hundred years old. The product is based on a regular payment structure, and simply pays out the value of the policy upon death.

WHOLE LIFE INSURANCE POLICY

Whole life insurance is available in two types of payment structures. You can have premiums that are paid until your death or premiums paid for a specified period of time or age, such as twenty years or until you turn sixty. Whatever method you choose, the coverage is lifelong and permanent.

In the beginning years of the policy, you pay more in premiums than the coverage actually requires; this is how the policy reserve is created. Over the years, this cash reserve increases and can act like a forced savings reserve fund. If you decide you no longer want the policy, you will receive these funds, referred to in the business as a "cash surrender value."

BEST CHOICE: APL AND ETI OPTIONS ON YOUR WHOLE LIFE POLICY

An automatic premium loan (APL) option on your policy means that if you forget to pay or cannot afford the premiums one month, the policy remains active and the payment will be made from your cash reserve fund. Extended term insurance (ETI) allows you to keep the policy active if, for any reason, you stop paying into the plan. The premiums will be drawn from your cash reserve fund; when the fund is depleted, the coverage will be cancelled.

UNIVERSAL LIFE INSURANCE POLICY

This type of permanent insurance can be an excellent tool for tax and estate planning. It provides for a structured insurance benefit with an investment account that you can personally control. Like whole life insurance, a universal policy has a cash account value that can grow without restrictions based on the return on your investments. This policy is also among the most flexible and ultimately has the most risk. You are responsible for the investment decisions in the policy; if the plan performs well, you might be able to stop making your premiums and take out the surplus in your cash account. Conversely, if the investment goes down, you could find yourself reducing the death benefit or making up for the losses from your personal savings.

BEST CHOICE: UNBUNDLING YOUR UNIVERSAL LIFE POLICY

A universal policy has three distinct components: the investment, the insurance, and the expenses. By unbundling these key elements of the policy, you will see the exact costs of the insurance and its monthly expenses. It is most important to have a true picture of your investment structure so that you can easily make modifications to your plan and your investments, and monitor the growth in your account.

When thinking of insurance, there are only three risks of financial loss—death, disability, and old age. You must continually revisit and measure your risks to re-evaluate your insurance. Insurance can be expensive, and it is obvious that you need it when you are young, just starting out, or have a family with young children. As you age and accumulate wealth, it might not be as important to provide for dependents who are now married and have moved out. Avoid the temptation to put your plan on autopilot, and make sure that you don't limit your plans only to life insurance as you get older.

Planning for the future should include planning for unexpected events. It is important to have a Will when you die, but also to have a Power of Attorney and a Living Will in case you become ill or disabled. One third of Americans and Canadians ages thirty-five or older will suffer a disability lasting at least six months before they reach sixty-five. Of those who suffer a disability, between thirty-five and sixty-five, half will have the disability for five years or more, and nearly a third will be disabled for life.

It is important for you to have a well-thought-out strategy that provides for the loss of income and protection against the unexpected. Don't make foolish decisions not to protect your family and your assets to save a couple of dollars. It is not worth it. Do your homework and explore all options for disability and life insurance. Do not leave yourself unprotected. This is the basis of protecting your CORE. It is important to revisit your needs every five years so that you always keep your budget tight, lean, and on track at all times.

CLIENT STORIES:

Divorced, Separated, and Starting Over

STARTING OVER CAN BE VERY HARD ON YOU PERSONALLY, LET ALONE financially. Having to accept the stress of a divorce with or without children can be traumatic, and will usually affect our lives forever. It is easy to let your finances take a back seat to your future planning, since retirement is generally viewed as a "couple" event. The reality of having to plan on your own can be challenging, and often creates too much complexity at a time when you need simply to bring some order to your life. Most new singles are left feeling unsure about how much money they will need at retirement, and will need to step up their savings to secure their future.

Credit qualifications seem to be changing year after year, and what you were approved for with a partner four or five years ago might not be the same now that you are on your own. Lenders are much less lenient now than in the past, and simply are not taking any chances.

Either a separation or a dissolution agreement is needed when a couple splits. The banks need a separation agreement to outline the disbursement of all shared liabilities, loans, and mortgages. It will also provide clarification on alimony or child support payments and further outline the division of pensions, investments, and assets. A dissolution agreement is the same as a separation agreement except that it is mainly used for common law couples, roommates, or family members who purchased a property together.

For most newly separated clients, it is like starting over from the beginning. Unfortunately, today more and more middle-aged couples are finding that they have very little money to split with their ex once assets are liquidated and the mortgage and debts are paid out. It is important to reach inward and become stronger. Starting anew can and should be an empowering lifestyle adjustment, and most will face the challenges head-on and triumph. Here are the stories of clients who did just that. You can, too!

STAY-AT-HOME MOM STARTING OVER: CHARMAINE

I was standing in line at a hardware store when I heard my name being called. I looked back into a sea of busy shoppers and noticed a little woman making her way through the crowd toward me. I actually didn't recognize her at first, but once she spoke I knew exactly who she was. Charmaine had been one of my closest friends in high school, and I hadn't seen her in over twenty-five years. Since that reunion, we have spent a lot of time together. It was not hard to become good friends again.

Charmaine married young and gave up her career to stay at home with her four boys. She was a great mother and was very involved in her children's school, hockey, and soccer, and volunteered at her church. It always amazed me how much energy Charmaine had to do all the extracurricular events and run a household full of men. Her husband, Steve, was a production manager at a packaging company, and had just recently moved to a new employer for a slightly higher-paying position with more future potential. Life was good for this couple, until the day of Steve's car accident.

Steve was badly hurt and was off work for over three months. After his recovery, Steve would not return to work; instead, he collected disability for the next six months. Although he was physically fine, Steve went into a deep depression during his recovery and proclaimed that he would never be able to return to work. Charmaine tried everything to help her husband, but to no avail. Eventually, the disability payments stopped coming, and Steve's employer refused to hold his position.

Once the money stopped coming in, the bills began mounting with every passing month. Charmaine maxed out all their credit, and was devastated when her bank turned down a consolidation loan. After almost three years of exhausting all their savings and using all possible credit in the hope that Steve would break free from his depression, Charmaine had had enough. They were no longer able to make their mortgage payments, and would now have to sell their home. Steve and Charmaine legally separated. Charmaine and the boys moved into a rented townhouse close to their school and Steve moved back with his parents.

With only $46,000 left from her marriage of fifteen years, Charmaine would now have to start again, on her own, with four impressionable boys. It wasn't easy, but she triumphed in the face of adversity and loneliness. She was a very strong woman and started eliminating her negative thoughts by creating opportunities for her success. She didn't let her circumstances bring her down. Instead, she became empowered, and it was her unstoppable willpower that showed her boys first-hand how to get back on your feet and recommit to life.

Charmaine knew a lot of women, and began networking with all her friends and acquaintances, who were more than willing to help her in any way possible. She decided to open a small consignment shop in the quaint village where she lived. This was a huge risk for Charmaine, and she would be using up all of her savings on this venture; however, she was extremely committed. With her boys' encouragement and a giant leap of faith, she took the first steps toward her new life.

Now this was not just any consignment shop, it was a high-fashion diva boutique. All the merchandise had to be haute couture and have a designer label. She was not catering to the little old ladies who wanted to buy used clothing, but rather working professional women who wanted to find something unique, different, and high fashion, without the exorbitant price tag. She also sold jewellery, handbags, shoes, boots, scarves, and belts—everything for men and women.

It was an overnight success story. The store did very well and even won an award for best new business in her community. After four years, Charmaine opened her second store in another town, and has plans for a third store in another two years. Today, all of her boys are in college and she was able to help out each of them financially. She saved over $210,000 in investments and owns a small home free and clear, valued at $173,000. Charmaine is not only a friend, but a great example of someone who aspired for more out of her life and developed the resilience to turn her life around and become committed to success.

COACH'S MESSAGE

The key to Charmaine's self-achievements was that she kept her expenses low. Before opening her store, she worked at every job she could find. For the first six months, she worked part time at her church, a fast-food restaurant, and a housewares store. Charmaine became a voracious saver, and when she found a suitable store location, she haggled with the landlord for the best possible price, getting him to make structural changes and improvements at no cost. All four boys were very involved in the setup of her store, and she made sure each one had a hand in its success. Even today, Charmaine's boys are still involved in her business, and they have looked after her stores when she has gone on short vacations.

When Charmaine opened her first store, she kept costs down by painting the interior all in white and making all her own fixtures. The initial merchandise was provided by friends and acquaintances who were fine with not being paid or reimbursed for their clothing unless it sold. Charmaine became a meticulous record keeper and refused to use credit to fund her venture. She never overextended herself financially, and did not even buy her home until she had almost all of the funds to purchase it free and clear. She could have easily qualified for a mortgage or bought a much larger home using credit, but refused to, not wanting ever to go through her past experiences with debt.

Charmaine is an amazing role model for her boys, and they each have a profound work ethic after seeing how hard their mother struggled and how committed she became to her self-achievement and success for her family. Charmaine loves what she does, and is now happy every day. She made some tough choices, but always took the incremental steps to keep moving forward, and she made it. You can, too. Believe in your ability to become more, and you will.

ONE HAS THE MONEY, THE OTHER HAS THE INCOME: HELEN AND MARTIN

I met Helen through a mutual friend many years ago and helped her and her husband finance their home, set up their retirement portfolio, and establish an insurance solution for life and disability. Five years later,

Helen and her husband were divorcing, and she was buying another home with her new partner, Martin. Helen was forty-eight and had one teenage son who chose to live with his father; Martin was fifty-five, with three adult children. Helen was in the midst of finalizing her separation agreement when we first got together to discuss future financing. She was now quite happy with her life, and although her upcoming divorce would be difficult, they had been able to reach an amicable division of assets. After the sale of their matrimonial home and all assets were liquidated and liabilities paid, Helen would receive $320,000. She could also expect to receive $1,200 a month in alimony, and planned to keep working as a receptionist.

When we chatted about her plans for the future, it was necessary to review her separation agreement to determine the stipulations, if any, on her alimony. Now on her own, it was important to begin to set up a plan for her financial future. Women, on average, earn less than men but outlive them by five to ten years, and many single women don't know how much money they'll need at retirement. That being said, Helen was not interested in talking about retirement, and wanted to purchase a new home with Martin. So we put financial planning aside and focused on how best to secure her assets and purchase a new shared residence.

Helen's separation agreement had a cohabitation clause that stipulated that, if she were to cohabit or remarry, her alimony would cease. Her income of $22,500 would not be enough to qualify for a new mortgage. Helen and Martin wanted to purchase a new home for $430,000. They had decided that Helen would put down the deposit and Martin could qualify for the new mortgage since his income was $95,000. Martin was a sales manager at a large car dealership and currently rented an apartment close to work. He had never been married, and no longer paid child support since his children were now adults. Martin did not have any savings or investments, and felt this was a good arrangement for them both. As they put it, Martin brought the income and Helen brought the down payment.

Helen wanted to put down only 20% of the purchase, and agreed to pay the mortgage together with Martin. This is usually how clients and bankers will set up new mortgages, with banks interested only in acquiring the business and facilitating the transaction. Doing it this way, however, is truly not the best for either client. There is no clear division of the asset, and without a cohabitation agreement between Helen and Martin, there would be a lot of grey areas if they split. Martin most likely would end up paying more toward the monthly expenses since he clearly earned more.

Like most couples, these clients believed that, if they were to separate, they would just sell the property, and, after the debt was paid, Helen should get back her deposit. But what happens if one of them wants to stay and the other wants to sell? Would there be enough left over to pay back the original deposit? What happens if one dies and adult children force the sale to capture their inheritance? It is always prudent to remember that sometimes children can undermine a new couple's finances, making it all the more necessary to have things clearly defined in a financial agreement and in plain language.

SO WHAT DID THEY DO?

With most new adult relationships that involve money, especially if this is your second or third relationship, it is always better to have full financial clarity between the partners. You are not a young couple just starting out with nothing but love. Instead, you are bringing many facets to your new relationship, and are not as naive as you were the first time around. It is important for you and your partner to dispel any grey areas when it comes to your finances, so that you can concentrate on your new relationship and not let any ill-divided monetary grievances undermine your future together. We wanted the purchase of Helen and Martin's new home to be equally divided between the two of them, and we therefore set it up as follows.

First, we would have to account for closing costs, which would add an additional $8,500 based on their purchase of $430,000. The total cost of the house to be divided 50/50 therefore would be $438,500, or $219,250 each. We suggested that Helen pay her entire half share of the property and not be expected to contribute to the mortgage. This could easily be done using her settlement from her divorce. We would then set up a mortgage for the other half, which Martin would pay. Ownership of the property could be clearly defined, and Martin would take ownership of the outstanding debt in the form of his new mortgage. By setting up their purchase in this manner, Helen would be free to contribute to the other household expenses from her income, and would not have to help pay into a large mortgage. Her investment in the property was clearly defined, and she could take the balance of her divorce settlement and invest it for her future retirement.

We suggested that Martin take out a separate mortgage life and disability insurance policy on his loan so that, if he were to die, the debt would be paid out and Helen could sell the property to pass half over to his estate for his children. If they wanted, they could also go a step further and get additional life insurance on both, naming each other as beneficiaries. By doing this, they could eliminate the forced sale of the property if one were to die, and therefore allow the surviving partner enough funds to pay out half of the value of the property to their partner's estate and continue living in the property debt-free.

It was necessary for both to outline their wishes in a new cohabitation agreement and also update their Will and Power of Attorney. A cohabitation agreement can be a valuable tool, since both partners are on the title to the property and, therefore, by law both will be on the mortgage. Most couples overlook this, and find out at the last minute on closing. The rule is, if both clients are on title, they are both on the mortgage. The reasoning behind this is to ensure no additional charges or liens can be put on the property without the consent of all owners on title. One can easily outline the terms of the debt and percentage of ownership with a clearly defined cohabitation agreement.

Helen and Martin were pleased with the division of their purchase, and decided to get additional insurance for each other to make sure not only that they provided an inheritance for their children, but also protected each other in the event of the death of one. Martin also started a monthly contribution toward a balanced investment fund and added Helen to his benefits program with his employer. The cohabitation agreement is usually a major milestone to get over in new couple relationships, but Helen and Martin could clearly see the value and wanted a clean start to begin their lives together. They were well on their way to building their financial future together, and could now concentrate on their new home and each other.

COACH'S MESSAGE

Starting over can sometimes be a blessing and a wonderful new beginning. Now that you are older and more experienced, this time you need to make sure you protect your assets and never create uncertainty about your financial future. There are a lot more variables to consider when you are starting again, and you owe it to yourself and your family to clearly define Yours, Mine, and Ours.

Of course, if you are starting again with very few assets, then a prenuptial agreement or cohabitation agreement is not necessary. The agreement is only needed to provide for any future division of property in the event of a breakup. Agreements must favour both parties, and bring clarity to your union and your combined assets. Most people are reluctant to entertain even discussing a financial agreement for fear of acting insensitive or showing a lack of love toward their partner. Please do not view it this way. Instead, think of it as a framework that is best for your future together.

When it comes to money, it is best to view things like a banker: without emotion. Having your finances clearly defined relieves the anxiety and stress that might arise in the future. Plan today for a long life together.

WHY CAN'T I GET A BETTER MORTGAGE RATE? JULIE

I met Julie through a mutual friend and immediately liked her. She was a vibrant fifty-four-year-old, well spoken, and impeccably dressed. She had separated from her husband after twenty-nine years of marriage and was slowly putting back the pieces of her life. She was one step ahead of most newly single clients because she had already established a legal separation agreement with her ex-husband and completed the division of assets and liabilities. Their matrimonial home had been sold, and all shared liabilities had been paid out and closed. Julie received $530,000 from their split, and could expect monthly alimony of $3,300. She would not receive child support since their two daughters had moved out and were now attending school in another city. Julie had no other investments or savings and no prospects of any future pension.

To help out her daughters, Julie purchased a condo apartment close to the university they both attended. This took all of her settlement funds, but she felt this was a good long-term investment, since the girls agreed to pay a small amount of rent, which would cover the monthly condo fee and property taxes.

Julie rented a small apartment not far from my office. She supplemented her alimony with a home-based business selling professional dance costumes. Her daughters had been in professional dance competitions since they were three years old, and Julie had always designed and made beautiful dresses for their recitals. This was a cash business for Julie that helped provide a better standard of living.

After about a year, Julie decided that she wanted to purchase a small condo apartment, and felt it would be smarter for her to pay into a mortgage, rather than wasting her money on rent. The apartment she wanted to purchase was $365,000. With this purchase in mind, Julie met with me for advice on how to get approved and to understand why she had been declined by the three banks she had gone to for a mortgage.

Julie was hitting financial roadblocks for many reasons. First, she did not have any taxable income other than her alimony. This often happens with divorced women who have been out of the workforce for many years. Even very well-educated women who have been at home for a number of years find it tough to get a job again. Because Julie did not have employment income and was simply using her alimony and rental income from her girls, the banks declined her request for credit. Alimony must be thought of as a supplement to employment income because lending institutions will not use it on its own. Typically, banks will use only 60% of alimony and will want to add this to your employment income to mitigate the servicing on a new mortgage or loan. Julie could not understand why all the banks were doing this to her, since the government viewed it as full taxable income. Why couldn't the banks do the same?

The banks are all about reducing risk when they lend. Of course, all lenders are slightly different from one province to another, but as a standard practice most will only use 50–70% of alimony as income since there is no fallback or control over this support payment. What happens if the supporting spouse refuses to pay, declares bankruptcy, or even dies?

If the client has employment income in addition to the support payment, then the lender feels that this risk has been mitigated. Alimony alone is too risky for a lender to accept on any secured or unsecured loan, and is one more indication of the new rules and regulations now mandated to tighten the financial industry.

The second reason the banks were declining Julie was that she did not have any investments to strengthen the deal. She did have her condo, which her girls were renting, but this rental income could not be used because it was from her daughters, not from a legitimate tenant. Also, Julie was not declaring this rent on her taxes, and the little money that she did receive barely covered maintenance and taxes.

The third reason lenders were having a problem was that Julie did not have any credit history and had a very low beacon score on her credit bureau. For most of her life, Julie had used credit cards, but always as the co-applicant. Her husband was the primary applicant on all of her previous cards and loans. After their split, she was left with no credit. Because she had never looked after the money, it was difficult for Julie to adapt to her new financial lifestyle, and she opted to pay for things with cash. She only opened a bank account for rent payments and alimony deposits. She used her debit card and cash for all her purchases and never bothered to apply for or establish her own new credit.

We were able eventually to get Julie a mortgage on the condo she rented to her daughters. We found a secondary lender—not an A lender—that would provide a mortgage at 65% loan-to-value, giving her $345,000. This lender mitigates risk by charging a much higher rate of 6.49%. This rate on its own was not too bad, but when the A lenders were offering 3%, it was quite disappointing to Julie. There was also a mandatory lender administration fee of 1%, which would mean she would pay an additional $3,450 on closing along with legal fees and taxes.

SO WHAT DID SHE DO?

Julie was not happy with this solution. The $345,000 was not enough to cover the purchase of the condo she wanted, and she did not have any other cash to make up the difference or pay for the closing costs. She was very disappointed with the rate offering, and still felt that she was being penalized because she was a single, divorced woman.

It is very hard to understand the banking framework of lenders when you have not been used to dealing with them in the past. Julie's only experience up to now was opening an account, and it was really important for her to start building her credit for the future. We suggested that she start with a bank Visa or Mastercard and perhaps apply for a department store or gas card.

Julie decided that she would try to get a full-time job, and then planned to reapply to get a better lending rate. This proved to be a difficult task also. With no prior work experience, Julie found it a challenge to get a full-time job. After a couple of months I saw Julie again, and she now had a part-time position at a small retail store and could expect a minimum of ten hours per week.

The new credit cards and new part-time job definitely helped Julie begin her journey toward getting future credit from the banks, but they were still not able to provide her with what she needed to purchase the second condo. When we chatted about the monthly expenses that she would incur, she began to understand why the servicing ratios for her request were just too high. The mortgage payment would have been $2,335 per month, and she could expect to pay $430 for condo fees and $370 for taxes, utilities, and insurance. This would mean Julie's monthly expenses would come in at $3,135. With Julie's part-time income of $125 per week and alimony of $3,300, the banks could not justify the shortfall to mitigate future risk. If her alimony got delayed or disrupted for any reason, she would not be able to pay her monthly commitments.

As well, the TDS ratio, which was acceptable only at 42%, was far too high at a whopping 78% for this deal. I wanted Julie to think about the "bigger picture," not just about this moment with the condo purchase. It is sometimes hard to think ahead ten, fifteen, or twenty-five years from now, but it was so important for Julie to begin planning her future.

Rather than getting into debt, we recommended Julie keep her monthly expenses low and start investing for the long term. She was only fifty-four, and could continue working and saving for another ten years. If she were able to keep her expenses low, continue to live on her alimony, and invest her part-time income of $125 per week, she could expect to have approximately $82,680 in ten years. When her daughters graduated university in four years, Julie could sell the condo and use these funds to purchase her own condo without a mortgage. We also wanted her to consider a less costly purchase, so that the taxes and fees would be lower per month. The extra funds saved by purchasing for less could be added to her investment to continue growing for her long-term protection. With no debt, her home paid for, and a small retirement fund, Julie could secure a modest, comfortable lifestyle as she ages, with no worries in the future.

We projected her condo sale proceeds to come in at $613,200, and with the purchase of her new residence at $375,000 we anticipated adding $200,000 to the investment portfolio. At age sixty-five, Julie could expect to have a modest savings portfolio of approximately $414,820 and would continue to own her home free and clear. Her net worth would then be approximately $795,000.

COACH'S MESSAGE

Understanding financial institutions and their lending practices today can be very frustrating. Julie had come a long way from not knowing anything about banking and financial planning to building her own credit and savings for her future. Your own personal financial success does not have to be difficult or complicated. Once you begin to understand the basics of creating financial wealth, you can set yourself up for a comfortable and secure lifestyle. The key is to not rush in too fast, and above all, do not go too deep into credit if you are approaching retirement. Remember, you want to be debt-free and wealthy (or comfortable) at retirement, not saddled with debt and paying exorbitant interest payments.

We all deal with money every day and for something so common it can sometimes make very little sense. How to balance your budget, how to save, how much to spend, and what future decisions to make: these are the questions most new singles grapple with. When you are on your own, monetary decisions can seem overwhelming. It is so important to talk to your finance coach or advisor and seek several professional opinions so that you remove apprehension toward future financial planning.

There is no reason for you not to retire wealthy unless you hold yourself back. If you find yourself single again—now that you are One—it is all up to You. Make a difference. Make it count. Do it now. You have the power within you. Good luck!

CLEANED OUT THE SECOND TIME AROUND: CANDICE

Happily married for over twenty-five years, Candice never imagined that her perfect life would suddenly turn upside down. She worked at a small manufacturing company as a bookkeeper, and when her husband died of a heart attack, she was ill prepared for the life changes that were to come. Candice was forty-six, with two sons in high school.

Most people protect themselves from the inevitable financial risks resulting from death or injury by acquiring separate mortgage or life insurance. Candice did have mortgage insurance, which dissolved the debt on their home. However, because her husband had recently moved to a new employer and was still on probation at the time of his death, she did not receive any death benefits or additional insurance funds. They always felt that insurance was too expensive or that they probably would never need it, and therefore never opted for an additional outside plan other than what was provided by her husband's employer. Candice still had $42,000 in credit card debt and another $38,000 on their line of credit. She did not have the necessary funds to pay for the funeral, and asked her parents to loan her the $20,000 needed for her husband's burial.

Candice went back to work after six weeks and tried to create some sense of normalcy for herself and her boys. Other than a small widow's pension from her husband's previous employer, Candice had no savings, investments, or retirement plans. They had never really talked about retirement, and were always just trying to make ends meet and save for their sons' education. Even with the mortgage debt paid out, Candice was finding it very hard to maintain the monthly financial commitments. She simply did not earn enough to pay for the carrying costs of her outstanding debt and the household expenses. Torn by her unwavering desire to keep her boys in their family home and finding the money every month to keep food on the table, Candice began to sink further into debt. Her grief and depression grew with every passing week.

When I met with Candice, I recommended that she consider downsizing her home to alleviate the financial burden and allow her to begin saving for the future. This was not something that she wanted to consider at this time. She was dating a divorced man, also with two children, and thought it would be a good idea for them to combine their assets and help each other. I urged Candice not to enter into any relationship without a cohabitation agreement, but she felt this would put a dark cloud over their relationship and did not want to discuss this with her new partner, Anthony. She believed that Anthony was a great person and would be a much-needed role model for her sons. Anthony lived in a rented condo in the city, had a good income of approximately $110,000, and Candice believed he could help fill the void financially and emotionally. Anthony did not have custody of his children, but did pay child support and alimony.

I did not see Candice again for another four years. She and Anthony were no longer together, and she was in dire need of financial assistance. She looked completely worn out and had a weary sadness to her demeanour. The enormity of her situation was weighing on her, and she was in desperate need of legal counsel and a solution to her predicament.

Anthony had an abusive personality, which was more evident once he moved in and became financially entwined in Candice's life. Candice agreed to put Anthony on title to her property in order for them to take out a new mortgage for $280,000. The house was worth $352,000, and Anthony convinced Candice that they needed the new mortgage to pay off her debt of $102,000 and his debt of $78,000. The additional monies could be used to upgrade the home, go on trips, and purchase a new vehicle to replace Anthony's older truck.

Blended families sometimes look quite healthy at a distance, but most children do not adapt well to the change and can sometimes unknowingly undermine or put pressure on even the best adult relationships. This union was having a destructive end, as Candice now had to step into action to resolve her situation. She and her boys had moved out of her home and were living with her parents. Anthony was still living in her home, and she was unable to get him to agree to dissolve their relationship, sell the residence, and pay out their shared liabilities. Candice was working two jobs to make the minimum payments on her outstanding credit, and their mortgage payments were now in arrears. She was done chasing the fantasy that their relationship could be a unified family and now was resolved to being on her own, with the welfare of her boys her number one concern. Together they held a joint mortgage of $273,000, and Candice had an additional $14,500 in credit card debt and an overdraft loan of $3,200. She was now fifty-one years old, still working for the same employer, and making $38,600 per year. Her net worth was $18,300.

SO WHAT DID SHE DO?

This was a real dilemma for Candice, and she was advised by her lawyer to move back into her home, which she did. Her boys stayed with her parents, who luckily helped her out financially and provided great emotional support. Together we were able to get a very good lawyer for Candice who quickly forced the sale and division of assets to finally dissolve her relationship with Anthony.

Today Candice and her boys live in a small, two-bedroom rented apartment near her parents. She sold most of her furniture when she downsized to repay them. She plans to continue renting, and now saves 10% of her income in an emergency fund. She will continue to live close to her parents to provide support and care as they age, and can count on a modest inheritance of approximately $250,000 that will help her when she enters her latter years.

Adjusting your spending and creating a new lifestyle takes an enormous amount of courage and resolve. Candice is definitely a stronger and more independent woman than she once was, and has even begun a small, home-based business to fill her time and make more money. She always made beautiful handcrafted jewellery as a hobby, and has begun hosting home parties with friends to sell her creations.

COACH'S MESSAGE

Everyone deals with grief differently. Some widows will recoil and turn their back on the world, while others will seek out a replacement to fill the profound void in their life that has left them with a sense of cata-strophic loneliness. The wounds of divorce or death can be difficult for young adolescents, and the affects can last long into their adulthood, but families have the greatest gift of all: forgiveness. A family, however small, can provide great strength and support with an unwavering connection and love for one another that lasts through good and bad times. Candice had this and became a stronger person because of it.

Whether on your own due to death or divorce, never forget to plan for your future. Always step back to review your situation without emotions. Identify your strengths and list your assets. Begin to create a master plan that you can use as a guide to map out your future. Keep a daily Cash Journal. Talk to professionals and get support, financially, physically and emotionally. Start really believing in yourself, and give yourself the self-assurance to overcome your fears and attain the future you want for your family. Above all, protect your assets and your future.

Please review the Starting Over Checklist that follows. Right or wrong, this list was prepared by many divorced and widowed clients who felt these were the key points that helped them become more self-motivated and, most of all, got them back on their feet. You will make it. Be a fighter. Always protect yourself.

Good luck!

STARTING OVER CHECKLIST

WITH THE DIVORCE RATE IN NORTH AMERICA NOW CLOSE TO 40%, more and more people are experiencing a forced lifestyle change they were not prepared for. Paying child support and/or alimony can instantly lower your ability to service your old habits, and most divorced people will have to downsize substantially to accommodate their new commitments. Statistically, we have found that 80% of divorced men will find another partner to marry or cohabitate with. However, less than half of all single women find long-term partners. Most women, especially those over fifty-five, choose to stay single. No matter what your age, this is a time of great emotional upset when personal finances and retirement goals can easily be overlooked when customizing new life choices.

Remember, you must always have a plan. Even if your strategy changes, multiple times, always be planning your future. Develop the habit of forgiveness, and set yourself free to achieve great things for your new life and family. You cannot change what happened in the past, only what will happen in the future. Here is your chance to set things up in your personal and financial life the way you want them.

Focus on new accomplishments and future dreams. The following tips will help you get started.

Good luck!

POINTERS ON FINANCIAL WELL-BEING

1. If you never took care of the monthly bills and always left those decisions up to your partner, now you must make yourself more informed. Start by keeping a daily Cash Journal.
2. Make a list of all your assets.
3. Make a list of all shared liabilities to pay off and close, and determine what other liabilities you are going to be responsible for after your split. Create a financial budget for your new life. How much is needed for expenses and how much can you save? Articulate your plans for the future with your banker and ask for their help and advice.
4. Determine how much credit you can get. Can you stay in your home or does it have to be sold? Could you buy out your spouse to keep the family home?
5. Start establishing your own credit. Look at your credit bureau and have your banker explain it to you. Find out what your credit score is. Do you have to improve it?
6. Do not go out and get too much credit. You should never need more than two credit cards and a small personal line of credit.
7. Keep your job and build on your career. Try not to take on too much change until all the dust has settled.
8. Avoid starting a new business venture, a new job, or a new career unless you were planning for it long before your separation. Remember that changes to your income will affect your ability to

obtain new credit with lending institutions and could also jeopardize your current financial commitments. Always talk to your banker before making an adjustment to your income.

9. Find your own legal counsel. Do not share a lawyer with your ex.

10. Make sure your separation agreement is clearly defined. Sometimes it will have to be amended many times before it can be agreed upon. Remember, when there is more clarity, there is less stress.

11. If you are a stay-at-home spouse, never belittle your part of the relationship because you were not in the workforce. Child care is expensive and very important. Never resort to lessening your contribution to the family.

12. Don't sell the family home until you both have somewhere to go. Make sure both parties have their financial situation set up before you split and liquidate the family home.

13. When establishing support payments, most lawyers will use your previous year's tax return or a current paystub to determine your income. This is fine if you have a fixed salary. However, if you are self-employed, on commission, or paid through a variable compensation arrangement, it is best to use a three-year average to determine income. Annual bonuses should also be calculated based on a rolling three-year average.

14. Find a really good lawyer to help you set up a family trust, a new Will, and a new Power of Attorney. Clearly define your wishes, and make sure children are taken care of through legally documented guardianship and financial assistance.

15. Speak to a licensed insurance advisor to explore your personal insurance. Consider mortgage insurance to provide security for your children should you pass away. Make sure you have disability insurance to provide financial support if you cannot work in the future. It is so necessary for you to take care of yourself now that you are on your own.

16. Review your investment portfolio with your advisor, and plan for your future. Don't keep the same advisor as your ex. Make sure to establish new beneficiaries for your investments. If your children are young and will be under the care of a guardian should you die, consider having a different person managing the financial estate. This can be done with a family trust, a relative, or your advisor, who will have specific instructions on how to manage the investments and set up funds for education and annual allowances for care. Talk to your lawyer, accountant, and investment advisor to make sure you have made the best choices for you and your children.

17. Consider creating a family trust for the protection of minor children and assets. You might also wish to "freeze" your estate with a living trust, so that all asset growth and future capital gains are taxed in the hands of the beneficiaries, usually at a lower marginal tax rate. Remember that trusts do not last forever, and you should always seek professional advice if you are considering any type of trust to protect assets. They can be costly and sometimes very complicated, involving additional legal and accounting fees. Here is an example of a simple family trust. One of my clients, a well-educated, professional working woman, decided to set up a basic revocable family trust now that she was divorced. She had four children, and included their family home in the trust. The home ownership was divided into 50% ownership by the trust and 50% by the mother. If the mother remarried again and did not have a marriage contract, her new partner would be legally entitled to only half of her 50% ownership, or 25% of the asset.

18. Consider a prenuptial or marriage contract when starting again. Whether you have millions or just a couple of thousand in assets, having a well-defined contract eliminates any future confusion and clearly establishes Yours, Mine, and Ours.

19. Try to keep kids out of your financial decisions. Often, if your children are young adults or teens, it is okay to give them choices about the timing of certain changes, such as when to move or sell a home. Empowering your children and allowing them to help make minor decisions often softens the blow of an already-hard situation.

20. Try to stay happy. Most of all, keep it in perspective. Lots of marriages fail. Over time you will be able to move on and get stronger. If you have children, you know you need to. I promise it will get easier with time. You will make it!

POINTERS ON PERSONAL WELL-BEING

This is a book about you and your financial well-being, with the main focus on how to get you debt-free and wealthy. Reducing stress and learning to cope with your life and career will make you all the more comfortable taking the necessary financial decisions for your future. Here are some pointers to help you on your road to change and personal growth. You can do it!

1. Keep your closest friends, but make new ones, too. Join a social group outside your inner circle of married friends to build up your self-worth. Sometimes old friends will get tired of always hearing about the same thing, especially if they are married and can't relate. New people with new views and different perspectives can often give you a different outlook on life and make you happier.

2. Choose your battles with everyone: kids, friends, family, and strangers. Don't create too much stress for yourself—it's not worth it. Sometimes you just need to let things go or even ignore them. Try to meditate to create a sense of inner peace and calmness.

3. Consider chatting with a professional therapist. It is sometimes good to have a fresh new perspective on your situation from someone who is impartial and has nothing to lose or gain.

4. Try not to rely exclusively on family and friends for decision making, because they tend to take sides.

5. Consider having your children talk to a professional therapist, too, so that they are better equipped to work through their emotions. Talk to your child's teacher or counsellor at school so that they are aware of the situation and can provide support if needed.

6. Explore new interests. Consider going to church to make new friends and gain spiritual support.

7. Take a course at your local community college to upgrade your education or learn a new skill. Consider courses that challenge and inspire you. How about learning auto mechanics and repair, creative writing, or scuba diving? It really doesn't matter what it is, just as long as you are getting out there and experiencing new things.

8. Be a friend to yourself. Buy yourself something for just getting through a rough day. Treat yourself to something you have always wanted, like a special golf club or a spa day.

9. Join a workout or fitness class. You could also consider getting involved in an organized sport such as hockey, soccer, racketball, or tennis. There are many adult groups that play in the evenings or on weekends, and it is a great way to burn off stress, make new friends, and stay fit.

10. Try meditation. Always try to keep your stress down and find ways to lower anxiety to keep your body and mind strong. Remember to eat right. Take a daily vitamin supplement and consider speaking to a dietician to detox your body.

11. Let your doctor know what you are going through. Have a full physical and talk to your doctor about how you can improve your health if needed.

12. Make sure to get enough sleep. Sleeping can speed up your recovery and your ability to handle new challenges. Try to sleep at least seven to eight hours every night.
13. Get a pet. Become a new "mommy" to a cat, dog, bird, or whatever!
14. Do not tell everyone about your troubles. Your neighbours or co-workers don't need to know everything, and you certainly don't want to be the gossip around town or at the proverbial water cooler. Remember, keep your stress low.
15. Above all, never beat yourself up or take on the mental burden of your loss. Get dressed up. Go out. Keep yourself in the game, even if you don't plan to play. Only you can make yourself happy again, one day at a time.

Remember, you will get through this, and things will get better. You are strong enough!

CLIENT STORIES:

Already Retired or Only Five Years to Go

I CANNOT STRESS ENOUGH TO ANYONE READING THIS BOOK THAT YOU must stack the odds in your favour by planning for your future. The vast majority of clients only seriously begin planning for retirement when they are five to eight years away from wrapping up their working career, and most are not sure how much money they really need. When time is running out, most people panic and begin to make risky investment choices to try to make up for their past lack of effort to lower debt and build wealth. This is when you need a finance coach and to seek the much-needed assistance to ensure you get to retirement debt-free and intact with a comfortable retirement fund. Yes, I said comfortable. It might not be millions, but if your debts are paid, you can live comfortably into old age. Above all, please remember that taking on too much risk to make up for lost time will be fatal to your finances, your lifestyle and your well-being.

Most clients do not make their "hard stop" to retirement until well into their sixties or early seventies. Most will say that they "retired" at fifty-five or sixty, but we have found that more than 75% of retired clients go back to work. The return to the workforce is usually only on a part-time basis, either to keep busy or to inject a little extra income into their monthly budget.

Some people will make the right choices along the way, while others might be forced to make changes because they didn't save enough. If you are retired now or almost there, you will be inspired by the stories of people like you who have reached retirement. Some thought they had enough to retire on, and then found themselves with potential shortfalls and heartbroken by the thought of a future of dwindling assets. Here you can see for yourself how to retire comfortably and what to expect when retired. Right or wrong, you can assess how others have made changes and found their own retirement bliss. Here are some questions to consider when you are planning for your retirement.

1. What will your retirement look like?
2. Be honest with yourself: what will your future expenses be?
3. Are you going to be responsible for aging parents or children?
4. Envision what you plan to do after you stop working. How do you plan to pay for the retirement you are dreaming of?
5. If you become disabled, will you have enough money to live on? What about long-term care?

One thing is common among almost all new retirees: they all under-estimated the amount of funds needed at retirement and had a profound adjustment during the first year. As we noted earlier, many advisors call this the "Honeymoon Stage." This is the time when newly retired couples, still young and vibrant, burn through their money with a pent-up desire to travel and spend. After the first year, most will settle into a budgeted schedule. This is a good time to talk to your finance coach about your future "nonworking" plans day-to-day and how to plan for future travel, tax shelters, and long-term care if needed.

I have found that most people in their fifties, sixties, and even early seventies are not planning for long-term care and believe that they will be able to stay in their home well into their nineties, on their own and unassisted. I hope this is true for you, but the statistics say otherwise. Make sure to plan for the eventuality of assisted living, or at the very least discuss future care with your family. Never stop planning! It will always take the uncertainties out of your future.

WHAT HAPPENED? WE'RE NOT READY: ROSE AND PETER

In the early 1990s, the banks were offering mortgage rates at 10–12% and clients were haggling over quarter-points in the rates between lenders. Clients have now enjoyed very low financing for more than a decade, with lending rates hovering below 5%. Some clients don't even know what it would feel like to have a loan or mortgage at a double-digit rate. I see many clients extremely disappointed if they sign a mortgage at 3.10% and then find out their friends just signed for 2.95%. Both are amazing offers that my clients back in 1992 would have killed for.

The low-lending-rate landscape has brought a wave of credit availability for almost everyone, and many believe it has contributed to the overextended debt loads on the average family. It has also put a lot of pre-retirees at risk. Unlike the young, who have many years to recover, many couples now approaching retirement have taken advantage of the lower rates, overspent, and are now in trouble. When clients were renewing their mortgages, they were thrilled to see the lower rate offerings, and the banks were more than happy to provide more credit in the form of larger mortgages, lines of credit, overdraft protection on their bank accounts, and increased limits on credit cards. The ease of acquiring credit became almost an epidemic as banks continued to throw more money at any client they could qualify. Many pre-retirement couples decided to upgrade their homes, go on family trips, buy cars, and generally use their new-found credit availability to improve their lives.

Rose never worked outside the home, and her husband Peter worked for forty-three years at a large telecom company. At age sixty-five, Peter was forced to take retirement, but could count on a pension income of $48,000 a year. Peter had never contributed to his company's savings plan; however, he planned to use the government supplementary pension programs, which would add an additional $13,500 to his annual income. Peter and Rose lived in the same home they purchased when they first got married. At the time, it cost only $23,000, and now was worth $575,000. They raised two wonderful children and they had five grandchildren who visited often. Life was good, but there was a cloud of uncertainty over their future retirement.

Rose and Peter had been referred to me through a mutual friend. We chatted about what they wanted in retirement and how they had prepared over the years. They had a mortgage of $482,000, their line of credit was over its limit at $38,145, and they had three credit cards with outstanding balances totalling $26,500 and a retail loan of $2,450. They recently had consolidated their two car loans into their mortgage and pushed the amortization back to twenty-five years. With Rose not working, it had been hard to save for the future. They had tried to invest on their own in the stock market, day trading without an advisor, but found that they lost more often than they gained. Their total savings amounted to $121,500. Their net worth was $147,405.

With their current debt load, they were finding it difficult to manage each month, and now with Peter's reduction in income, they were reaching to credit to supplement their lifestyle. Peter had been retired now for seven months, and had just recently been hired at their local hardware store part time. They said the extra monthly income would be helpful, and Rose believed it would keep Peter "out of trouble." They were a lovely couple, but in desperate need of a financial solution.

It was now necessary for Rose and Peter to eliminate their debt and learn to live day-to-day within their fixed income without going to credit for extra "must-haves" every month. The solution would most likely be drastic, but if they were not resolved to fixing their situation, we feared they would be forced to, by the banks, in less than a year. The monthly utility costs, property taxes, and mortgage payment already exceeded their after-tax income. There was not enough money for food and general living expenses or even the minimum payments on their other outstanding credit cards. Because they were continually late on their monthly bills, their credit ratings were falling, and the daily worry over money was definitely taking its toll on this couple. Peter had wondered if they should declare bankruptcy, and Rose was beside herself with worry. Something had to change.

SO WHAT DID THEY DO?

We recommended that Peter and Rose sell their home to dissolve their debt and move to adult rental accommodation. They lived in an area where there were many adult apartment facilities that catered to tenants over fifty years old. Most people do not consider renting; however, it should not be discounted when financial planning for your long-term retirement. Streamlining your expenses down to only one monthly rental fee can instantly make it easier for you to budget and live within a fixed pension income. Gone are the monthly expenses of owning a home, the maintenance and upkeep, the utilities and taxes. Simplifying your lifestyle helps remove the stress of extra expenses and makes it easier to lock and leave your apartment to enjoy other activities and travel.

We also suggested they downsize to only one vehicle to further lower expenses, since most apartments typically provide only one reserved parking spot. We wanted Rose to keep a daily Cash Journal of all expenditures, and showed her how to use the Finance Tracker. By always keeping a tally on monies coming in and out, you begin to change your spending habits. No one can ever force you to spend more or save more. It comes from your inevitable desire to want something. If you want more money, you must spend less and save it. It is really that simple. By keeping a Cash Tracker, you give yourself the proof you need to be able to buy now or wait until you have saved enough.

Rose and Peter wanted to break free from debt, and did sell their home for $580,000. After fees and taxes, they were able to net approximately $548,000 which was used to pay off all their debts. They were short approximately $3,000 that they still owed in credit card debt. With the sale of one vehicle, this debt was eliminated. They found a very affordable two-bedroom rental that would cost them $1,250 per month, and Rose already knew some of the other residents and began making plans. She decided to sell most of their furniture and completely furnish their new apartment in a more modern style. This became a new adventure as well as a new beginning for them both, and Rose was determined to make it fun. I have to say that she had great enthusiasm about their new debt-free life, and creatively organized their ideas and goals for their future.

We chose a compounding balanced fund for their savings of $121,500 with minimal risk to their capital and a return of at least 5.5%. This investment could expect to grow modestly to $196,781 within the next eight years. Peter planned to continue working part time for the next eight to ten years, and we wanted to ensure their investment could provide for any monetary assistance needed for long-term care.

With all expenses now eliminated, Rose found it easy to live on Peter's pension income. The money from the part-time job could now be saved for fun retirement plans, such as holidays, weekend getaways, and golf trips. For the first time in over forty years, they had no debt. They used cash for most purchases, and kept track of all their spending using their daily Cash Journal. They each had a new credit card with a low limit of $1,000 to be used only for emergency purposes.

Rose had made many new friends at her new community and was involved in many social clubs. She played bridge every day, and when Peter wasn't working, he was playing golf. They were planning their trips "on the cheap," as Rose called it—always sticking to her Finance Tracker. She logged every dollar that came in or out of their account, and became a diligent saver and budget-minded tracker. Most of all, they were now stress free and very happy. Finally, Rose and Peter felt in control of their money and their future. They had found their own comfortable retirement and, once and for all, had broken free from the monotony of credit.

COACH'S MESSAGE

The question might not be if there is enough money to retire on, but rather if you can even afford it at all. With investment portfolios pressured by market volatility, rising household debt, and a new budgeted lifestyle with a forced fixed income, most people nearing or in retirement are becoming more and more worried.

Some might find they need to set their projected retirement date back a few years and continue working so that they can continue to save. Reducing expectations, working longer hours, or even returning to work to fund the security we need as we get older are all becoming more of a reality for clients approaching sixty-five. Unfortunately, being inadequately prepared for retirement might result in your having to sell your home to supplement income or liquidating a debt load that has become too much to handle.

There is a big difference between someone who has only five years to retire versus someone at fifty with perhaps fifteen more years to go. Don't be overly optimistic if you are approaching retirement with debt, and always use common sense when securing your financial future. When we are young we think that retirement is an eternity away, and then one day we wake up and it is just around the corner with only a few years left to plan. Think about where you want to go, and delve deeper into your goals and dreams for the future. Your plan does not have to have mathematical exactness, but rather should be an arrangement of ideas that will construct your future. If you are in debt, please do not be discouraged if you feel you have hit bottom. Most of us never really learn anything until we have suffered a little. Now you will probably have more clarity about your goals, and have the persistence and determination to achieve them.

Remember, anything worth having starts with a strong and persistent desire. Always prepare for every facet of your life, and arouse your enthusiasm toward your goals. Create your own convictions and organize your thoughts and ideas for your retirement future. Consider getting a cork board in your bedroom or kitchen to pin up pictures and notes to help remind you every day of your goals to retirement.

Don't be swayed by the crowds of people marching to retirement begrudgingly accepting a life with debt. Stop what you are doing right now and imagine what life would be like with no money saved when you finally stop working. Remove the financial impediments in your life. No one rarely gets forced into debt, yet here we all are with lots of it. Only you can change things to spend less and save more. Don't put it off. Start now.

THE PITFALLS OF PLANNING TOO LATE: GRACE AND ARTHUR

After the financial crisis of 2008, many people withdrew their stock portfolios and mutual funds to take control of their money from their investment advisors, whom they ultimately blamed for their substantial losses. Many saw fifteen to twenty years of savings decimated by the market in a matter of days, reducing their portfolios to less than half their value overnight. Most who stayed in the market have now recovered, after what's been called one of the most difficult recoveries since the Great Depression. Still, there are others whose portfolios have never returned to their original highs..

Grace and Arthur were not happy with their investment portfolio, now worth just under $400,000. They still had a mortgage after downsizing to reduce debt of approximately $338,000 and $53,000 on a personal line of credit. Arthur was sixty-one and Grace was fifty-six. Both had been previously married and each had adult children. They were a perfect match for each other and were very happy together. They had excellent careers, made very good incomes, and filled their spare time with travelling to exotic places and adding to their antique collections. Arthur was the CEO of a large construction company and made $250,000, while Grace was a VP of a mid-sized service company and earned $190,000.

I first met Grace and Arthur when they attended a seminar we were giving to help clients consider alternatives to investing in the stock market. The seminar was about investing in real estate and how clients could monetize their money and plan for their retirement. We encouraged clients to consider buying into the stock market as well as the real estate market while prices were low to capitalize on potential future gains. It was an inspiring event, with many professionals from all over the country offering their advice and insights.

The next time I met with Grace and Arthur was about four months later. They wanted to get together to talk about financing options. They had purchased three brand new executive townhouses and would need financing when they closed in less than six months. Arthur had decided he did not have time to start off with only one rental, but instead bought three homes from the same builder. This would pose a future problem. Not only did he purchase the properties without being pre-qualified; it was clear to the builder that he was purchasing the properties as investments and therefore would be subject to additional fees and taxes. When a new purchase is made through a builder and it is deemed to be owner occupied, the builder is obligated to pay for many of the extra taxes and fees. If, however, the home is purchased as an investment and future rental property, the builder can pass on these expenses directly to the purchaser. These were costs the couple did not anticipate. It is imperative that you do your homework, especially when you sign contracts for future financial commitments.

Upset with his poor-performing stock portfolio and feelings of desperation about retirement, Arthur felt the purchase of these townhouses was a surefire way to secure his future. He believed if he purchased them and rented them out, he could have the renters pay down the mortgages. Believing that the rentals would double in value, the plan was to sell them and make a great profit to wipe out his debt, ultimately giving him a better return than his current languishing stock portfolio. This sounded logical, but there are a lot of variables to consider when buying an investment property, and this turned into a very risky situation for Arthur and Grace. Because of their age and current debt, it was mandatory that they make very secure and prudent choices when investing, since there was limited time to recover from poor money-management decisions.

Taking into account their investments, debts, and current home value of $710,000, Grace and Arthur had a net worth of $719,000. Instead of purchasing investment properties, this couple should have concentrated on paying off their mortgage and line of credit by the time they planned to stop working. With their above-average incomes, they could have done this, but now it was necessary to completely restructure their holdings. Here is what we did to accommodate the three new real estate purchases.

The three rental properties were purchased for $380,000, $375,000, and $395,000 respectively. Each would need a mortgage at 80% loan-to-value, and the balance of the funds would have to come from refinancing their primary residence. It was necessary to refinance their current home immediately in order to provide the deposits requested by the builder before the properties closed.

Rental 1:
Purchase price = $380,000
New mortgage = $304,000 (80%)
Funds from refinance = $76,000

Rental 2:
Purchase price = $375,000
New mortgage = $300,000 (80%)
Funds from refinance = $75,000

Rental 3:
Purchase price = $395,000
New mortgage = $316,000 (80%)
Funds from refinance = $79,000

Total needed from refinance = $230,000
New refinanced mortgage on primary residence = $568,000 (80%)
Outstanding balance = $338,000 + rental properties $230,000

In addition to this new credit, there was still a remaining balance of $53,000 on their personal line of credit. The closing costs, taxes, and legal and builder's fees would total an additional $171,794. Because our clients lived in Ontario and these purchases were investment properties, the builder charged the HST costs for each property on closing. These unplanned costs could not be refinanced, and with no additional extension of credit the clients would have to cash in part of their stock portfolio to pay for these expenses. Their net worth was now **NEGATIVE** –$602,700, and they had $1,541,000 in outstanding debt.

Arthur had a great plan to build wealth for his future, but being impulsive without considering the potential obstacles and repercussions would prove to be a big mistake. Once the properties closed, it was harder than anticipated to procure suitable renters. It seems that most of the townhouses in this development had been purchased by would-be investors, and many were now for rent. It quickly became a tenant's dream. Vendors were frantic to get their units rented, and began dropping monthly rent costs to entice people to sign a lease. Grace and Arthur eventually were able to rent all three properties, but the rental income would fall short of covering the cost of the mortgages and property taxes.

SO WHAT DID THEY DO?

Now that the properties were rented and the dust had settled, it was important for Grace and Arthur to concentrate on paying down their current debt, the line of credit, and their new mortgage of $568,000. Their monthly cash flow was now very tight; however, the clients felt that their plan would pay off when they sold the rentals in five years' time. We put their remaining stock portfolio, now worth $226,000, into a more secure fixed income investment. As long as there were no surprises, their mortgage balances in five years would be down to the following amounts:

Primary residence = $485,000
Estimated projected value = $800,000

Rental 1 = $260,000
Clients' projected value = $485,000

Rental 2 = $256,000
Clients' projected value = $478,000

Rental 3 = $270,000
Clients' projected value = $503,000

There were a lot of "future projections" on the value of these rentals, and because of the clients' ages they had limited time to recover if the properties decreased in value. Investing in real estate can be a very lucrative venture, but you must consider all potential obstacles and be able to allow for additional time if needed. By holding onto the properties longer, the clients could continue to have tenants pay down the mortgage debt while the property values eventually increased to the necessary amount to justify a profit once sold. You also need to account for capital gains tax and legal and real estate fees that will lower your overall profit from the sales of rental properties.

THIRTY-SIX MONTHS LATER

Unfortunately, this retirement plan did not work out for these clients, and there is no happy ending here. Grace and Arthur found it very difficult to continue their lifestyle, and were short on cash every month. They were able to get an unsecured personal line of credit from another lender, and it was now over its limit of $75,000. They had simply too much debt and not enough funds to pay all the expenses.

Faced with the agonizing day-to-day monetary stress, Arthur decided to quit his job and accept a similar position at another company for $25,000 more. He was now making $275,000. This new position turned out to be a poor fit for Arthur, and within six months he would find himself unemployed. Looking for an executive position at the age of sixty-four is not easy. He was able to find the odd monthly contracting job, but for the most part Arthur was now forced into an early retirement. The financial burden would fall on Grace, and this would put a tremendous strain on their relationship.

The rental properties had to be sold. This was a hard pill to swallow for this couple, since they had tried so hard to create a "get-rich scheme" with investment properties. Fortunately, it did not take long to sell them, and after all the fees, taxes, and mortgage debts were paid, Grace and Arthur would be left with $295,000 still owing on their primary home, including the lines of credit for $75,000 and $55,000. The monthly financial drain was finally eliminated, and they could begin slowly to build some sense of normality back into their lives. Their investment portfolio was worth $274,700. Arthur did not have a pension, but planned to continue working part time with consulting positions as they became available. Grace was still working, and could expect a good pension of $5,500 per month once she retired in six years at age sixty-five.

We recommended that they downsize again to eliminate their debt, and they agreed. Grace had lived in an apartment for most of her life and wanted to retire to a small condo. Arthur had always hated this idea, but now decided it would be a good move for them. They sold their home and found a lovely condo apartment about thirty minutes outside the city. They were able to purchase their new residence free and clear, and after all the expenses were paid they could start over with no mortgage and no outstanding debt. With lower monthly costs, they now continued to save, and started to enjoy travelling again. Their net worth was $725,000, which included their condo value of approximately $450,000 plus their investments of $275,000.

COACH'S MESSAGE

The average retirement lasts twenty-five to thirty years. Beginning your nonworking years with little to no debt vastly increases the chances of having enough money to live on. If you are in your sixties, it is important for you not to consider anything too risky. Avoid at all costs get-rich schemes that put you and your hard-earned capital at risk.

I have seen very successful men and women like Grace and Arthur start companies or business ventures in their mid- to late sixties only to be overwhelmed by unforeseen obstacles, heightened personal stress, and increased financial burden. Jumping in too early and too fast without having the time to recover from a potential loss is a disaster waiting to happen. We often hear or read about the occasional success story, but I need to caution you here: do not take on too much undue risk. Sometimes a simple unforeseen turn of events can create a snowball effect that can be devastating and life changing. Be very careful when you are getting closer to your mid-sixties. You want to glide into retirement and have a nice, safe, soft landing with security and comfort. Avoid the bumpy ride to your latter years. We want you to be happy about retiring, not demoralized, defeated, and recovering from a beaten-down ego and investment portfolio.

My advice is **NOT** to take on any new ventures or monetary schemes if you are in your sixties. Risky ventures are for the young, who have the time to recover and get over it. Be careful. If you must try a new pursuit, above all do your homework and talk to your banker, investment advisor, accountant, or finance coach. Understand all the potential risks, and then make sure you are truly comfortable before you jump in.

Good luck!

CONSIDERING A SECOND CAREER IN RETIREMENT: DERRICK AND MARY-ANNE

Gone are the days of making a "hard stop" to a career and entering retirement. Almost 70% of newly retired people re-enter the workforce. Some start a new business venture they have always dreamed of, others return part time, while still others are starting a new career. Many newly retired clients find they are really not ready to sit around and do nothing. They are healthy, vibrant, and bring a depth of knowledge to a new industry positions that is unmatched by the young. Employers are always willing to pay for talent and see this shift in aging consultants as a welcome complement to their business.

The transition period to retirement can be very beneficial to clients wanting to continue generating income for additional savings or to extinguish outstanding debt. It is also very helpful in delaying withdrawals from an investment fund to allow assets to continue to grow. A retirement date is one of the most crucial elements of your final plan, and has a direct bearing on how much money you will have and, of course, how long those funds will last.

Derrick had just turned fifty-eight years old and was soon to retire from the police force after thirty-five years with a full pension. He had joined the force when he was twenty-three, and always loved the variety and challenge the role provided. His wife, Mary-Anne, was sixty-one, an elementary teacher, and still worked full time. Even though neither of them contributed to a pension plan, both would retire with an above-average pension income by today's standards.

Derrick and Mary-Anne had four adult children and six grandchildren. They had made sure to take a holiday together every year for the past twenty years, and were quite content to retire in their family home, which they had recently renovated. Their mortgage was not paid off yet, and together with the home upgrades had over $238,000 in a mortgage and line of credit. Their savings consisted only of their "rainy day" fund of $12,600, and most of their equity was tied up in their home, valued at $485,000. Their net worth was $260,000.

When we chatted about their plans for retirement, my initial concern was the monthly payments needed to satisfy the outstanding debt and how this would inevitably take a big chunk out of their fixed pension incomes. With no other savings to fall back on and no life insurance, it was imperative that they eliminate the debt if they wanted to retire. Mary-Anne did not want to work anymore, and was planning to retire at the end of the year. When I asked them how they planned to live day-to-day on less than half their current incomes, they were unsure. It seems they had always believed it would be fine when they finished working because of their guaranteed government pension income.

I carefully discussed with them that there honestly would not be enough funds for all current living expenses or any kind of major reduction in their existing debt load. What would happen if they needed a new car, a major home repair, or wanted to go away on those great vacation holidays they so enjoyed? They weren't sure. I had the answer, but the question remained: were they were willing to do what had to be done?

With more and more clients living well into their nineties, this couple most likely would go deeper into debt to make up for small, necessary lifestyle purchases. They eventually would have to sell their home to pay off the debt, and use the remaining funds for extended health care and living costs. They might have to consider renting an apartment, and would have very little to give their four children as an inheritance.

SO WHAT DID THEY DO?

It was necessary for them to understand how much money they would need if they retired now. We made a simple chart that showed how much income they could expect from their pensions, and then deducted all the necessary expenses, taxes, debt payments, food, utilities, and so on. We did not include any extras, such as gifts, entertainment, or personal items. It was clear that they would have a substantial shortfall just with the basic expenditures, and could easily see that they could not retire at this time. They had to make it a priority to eliminate their debt.

Our solution was not going to be favoured by Mary-Anne, who wanted to retire immediately. However, because of their lack of savings, it was mandatory that they both keep working. We chatted at length with Mary-Anne, who was feeling a little burned-out from her long teaching career; however, we wanted her to continue working for another five to six years until she reached sixty-seven.

Asking Mary-Anne to continue working became a big pill to swallow, but she knew it ultimately made sense and would help them eliminate their mortgage. There was a lot of discussion about what they should have done differently, but they both knew now that they had to put in that last push to the finish line before they could make their hard stop and retire. We suggested that Derrick also keep working until he reached sixty-seven, which would mean staying in the workforce for another nine years. Because Derrick could leave his current job now with a full pension, we suggested he do so and consider switching careers in the same field. Many of Derrick's colleagues had found second careers in fraud prevention and investigation with many major lending institutions, and Derrick had an opportunity to do the same.

If Derrick switched careers, he could take advantage of a permanent full-time income while still receiving his monthly pension allowance. This pension income could then be directed toward their outstanding debt to help pay it off faster. We would also want them to start living entirely on Mary-Anne's income, and with the debt payments now taken care of by Derrick's salary and pension, it should be easy for them to do so. By learning to live on one fixed income, they could develop the much-needed skills they would soon need when in retirement.

Derrick's income would include a $65,000 salary and pension allowance of $45,000 per year. This would mean, after taxes and deductions, we could put approximately $5,298 per month toward debt reduction and have the $238,000 completely paid off in just over four years. By the fifth year, when Mary-Anne would be considering retiring, not only would they have learned how to live on a new budget; they would have eliminated their debt and could own their home free and clear.

They agreed to embrace this solution, and we suggested we get together every six months to revisit their plan and review their progress. Sometimes it is necessary to have regular check-in meetings with your finance coach, who can give you pointers, support your efforts, and basically keep you on track. At every visit, we reviewed their budget, found ways to tackle unforeseen expenses, and provided a new net worth statement and revised financial plan to monitor increasing progress. At these sessions, it was decided that, when Mary-Anne retired and the debt was paid, they should downsize their home. The monthly expenses were going to be too high, and Mary-Anne wanted to try to continue to live on their pension income so that they could save Derrick's salary until he stopped working. This was a great idea, and one that we would work on together.

Before Mary-Anne retired, they sold their home for $558,000 and purchased a new residence for $321,000. After real estate fees, taxes, and expenses, they had approximately $200,000 to put into a savings plan. With no debt and lower monthly expenses, Derrick and Mary-Anne would live on their combined pension incomes. Derrick continued to work for another five years, and his income was added to their savings on a monthly basis. We chose a low-risk balanced fund for their $200,000 and added Derrick's monthly deposits to the growing investment. When Derrick finally ended his work career five years later, at sixty-eight, their savings portfolio totalled $508,042 and their net worth was now $883,000.

This couple had completely turned things around and rescued themselves. They had no debt, a sizable investment portfolio to draw from for future expenses or health care, and could live in their new home debt-free. They could even start travelling again, and had the budgeting tools to plan for their future expenditures. They also avoided the fate of having to move to a rental apartment, but could use their home as a tax-free inheritance for their children.

This was a huge lifestyle change, and there were many major adjustments for this couple. However, they executed their plan perfectly. They were very focused and committed. Derrick and Mary-Anne continually found ways to make improvements and ultimately secured their future in a very short time frame. Bravo!

COACH'S MESSAGE

Most people get consumed by failures in their personal finances. They mentally beat themselves up and think they should have more. Stop the pity party! Everyone has setbacks in their lives. Start supporting yourself, and commend yourself for now wanting to fix things for the better. Once you turn the focus back to the basics, you will start to see how easy it really is. Concentrate on positive ideas for change, and find opportunities that will help lower debt and create savings. There are opportunities all around us; we just have to be open enough to see them and make a plan to act on them.

Derrick and Mary-Anne did just that. They became open to new ways to make money and postponed retirement to guarantee the success of their personalized plan. They were focused on the future benefits and willing to make the necessary sacrifices. Having a quarterly review with your finance coach can also help provide a fresh perspective and new ideas, but more important, it will keep you on track and constantly moving forward.

Try not to dwell on the negative things too much. Sometimes people will dissect great opportunities, and eventually talk themselves out of everything that could make them successful. Always have a plan and work toward your goal. Dispel negative expectations that could become self-fulfilling prophecies. Focus on the benefits and stick to your time-table. You can do it.

With or without a finance coach, give yourself a financial review every six months. People think this is too old-fashioned or too difficult and complicated. Sorry, folks, to get out of debt you have to stop the spending and start the saving. By creating a budget that is tailored for your income and saving goals, you force yourself to get accustomed to a new lifestyle, one that is workable and personalized to you. Mary-Anne became a champion at budgeting, and even helped her adult children with their own plans. Remember, focus on the benefits and continually review and improve your progress.

Consider switching careers or going back to school part time to increase your income. I am not saying that you need to become something completely different or break out of your comfort zone. Rather, explore opportunities in your field and broaden your outlook on future possibilities. Derrick had a great opportunity to retire with a full pension and experience a different career path with additional income.

Ask yourself: "What's my biggest asset?" Most right away will think it is their home, their savings and investment portfolio, their car, and so on. But it's not your possessions, it's YOU. Your ability to make money is your greatest asset. Even if you are in your sixties, do not discount your ability to continue to earn income.

Get a little tougher on yourself to save and not spend outside your budget. Become committed to your plan. You will get there, no matter when you start. Just make sure you do start! Why not today?

FORGET THE PLAN, WE CAN MAKE IT ON OUR OWN: DEBBIE AND GREG

Life is filled with risks and opportunities. We all must make a multitude of decisions throughout our lives and, good or bad, we must live with the outcome of our choices. Financial planning is designed to motivate clients to make changes, discuss trade-offs, and sometimes discuss difficult decisions that might be necessary to ensure a comfortable future. Your finance coach should help you ascertain real risks and be flexible concerning your needs. Most of all, your coach should partner with you to help balance your budget, spotting possible blow-ups and removing the risk to your family's finances.

Debbie and Greg were in need of financial suggestions to help them secure their future at the end of Greg's career, which we estimated to be in about eight years. I suggested that it may be necessary for Greg to keep working past the age of sixty-seven. However, his health was poor, and they both wanted a solution that would not warrant this as a necessity.

The primary detriment to creating wealth is low savings, and this couple had none. Greg was fifty-nine and a senior project manager for a large shipping company in beautiful British Columbia. Debbie was forty-one and a talented painter, sculptor, and artiste-extraordinaire. They were a lovely couple enjoying a lavish lifestyle, with grand vacations every year. Greg had been with his current employer for only the past four years, and was hoping to stay with them until his projected retirement at sixty-seven. He was compensated well, with a base income of $195,000 plus an annual bonus. Granted, a great income; however, his employer provided no employee pensions and only limited benefits.

This is a growing trend. Companies are now hiring new full-time employees and compensating them with slightly higher salaries in place of employee benefits—something that was simply unheard of just ten years ago. Prior to his current job, Greg had always held contract positions in the same field, and although he was always paid well, he never seemed to have enough money to save for his retirement. Greg had been married twice before, and we were pleased to hear that he no longer paid alimony or support, so we could count on his entire income when devising a new solution.

Debbie had no taxable income, and mainly concentrated on artist commissions paid in cash. Their only asset was their home, worth $1,100,000. They had no RSPs, no pensions, and no savings. Their debt consisted of a $350,000 mortgage, a secured line of credit at $89,000, various credit card balances totalling approximately $17,000, and a monthly car payment for Debbie's new Mini. Their net worth of $630,000 was based solely on the estimated equity in their home.

When you are closer to retirement and have little to no savings, most people panic. You will need to review every aspect of your future wants. Your plans and wishes might have to be drastically modified to provide the necessary income you will need for day-to-day living expenses and eventual long-term care.

Greg was a very smart man; however, he never saw the value in meeting with a finance coach to discuss retirement, and he now knew he had to start saving for their future. Always putting it off and living for the moment proved to be one of his biggest regrets. With only eight years to go, we wanted to discuss how they planned to make ends meet. Greg would no longer have his above-average income, and with no savings, did they plan to sell their home? Would they rent an apartment to live on the sale proceeds?

We were very concerned about the lack of income, and asked again if Greg would keep working after sixty-seven, perhaps even on a contract basis. He did not want to. We advised them that Greg could only expect to receive approximately $18,000 a year from OAS and CPP, which Debbie would not be entitled to yet as she would still be only in her forties. This was surely not enough for their lifestyle. Was Debbie planning to support them once Greg stopped working? This, we soon realized, was also a NO.

For every problem, there is always a solution. However, perceived needs and wants sometimes have a way of completely knocking you off course. Ultimately, we all have the choice to do as we wish, and sometimes the best-made plans can find a way to overextend ourselves. Clearly, taking on too much risk when you are over sixty is a recipe for failure, although many feel it is necessary to make up for a lack of time. We all agreed on a well-thought-out personalized solution, but at the last minute our clients changed their minds. Let's see what happened.

SO WHAT DID THEY DO?

We recommended that they sell their home to dissolve their debt and slowly begin downsizing their lifestyle. We did not want them to make drastic changes all at once, and suggested they continue travelling, albeit on a slightly leaner budget. We had their home appraised, and suggested they could expect to sell for $1,150,000. We wanted them to consider selling to eliminate their debt, set up a new savings plan, and, of course, get them into a good home that they could own mortgage free by the time Greg retired.

With only eight years to plan, it was imperative that we begin a secured savings portfolio as soon as possible. Perhaps, once this plan was set up, Greg would be more motivated to put in monthly contributions for increased growth. We chose a compounding fixed income structure that could secure their capital and would provide them a guaranteed monthly retirement income when they were ready.

Both Greg and Debbie were fine about selling their home, and had been thinking of making a change for some time now. We chatted about lowering their next purchase to a price of no more than $600,000. They were a little unhappy with this low amount, but were resigned at least to considering what was available in this price range.

Debbie took on the task of looking for a new home and became quite excited about prospective homes outside the city that fit their new budget. Some even had the potential for an outdoor art studio to accommodate her work. Buying a home in a more rural community would add to Greg's commute, but he seemed to be warming up to the idea.

Here is how we estimated their solution.

$1,150,000	**Estimated sale of current residence**
(61,000)	**Less real estate fees and estimated legal costs**
(350,000)	**Pay off current high-interest mortgage**
(89,000)	**Pay off line of credit**
(17,000)	**Pay off credit cards**
(21,000)	**Pay off Debbie's car loan**
(10,000)	**Less estimated land transfer tax on a purchase**
$602,000	**Proceeds from sale**

Now using their funds from the sale, we estimated how to divide the proceeds between the purchase of a new home and an investment portfolio. It was important to start an investment plan so that we could capitalize on compounded growth, and the mortgage we would set up could be paid in the eight years remaining until Greg's retirement.

$602,000	**Proceeds from sale**
(350,000)	**Less funds toward their new home purchase**
(250,000)	**Less funds toward a new savings plan**

$600,000   Estimated purchase, monthly taxes = $340

(350,000)   Less funds from sale

$250,000   New mortgage at 3%, amortized over 8 years ($2,930
            per month)**

** *Mortgage paid at end of eighth year.*

** *Total estimated interest paid over 8 years = $31,307.*

** *$250,000 from sale toward new compounded fixed income savings*
portfolio at 5.671% over 8 years with estimated return of $410,850.
Estimated net worth at retirement = $1,075,000.

In short: no debt, with lower property taxes and lower home expenses. Debbie's artist commissions could be used to provide monthly cash income in addition to their government pension allowances.

The monthly mortgage payment of $2,930 for their new home was well within their budget and would not cramp their lifestyle. They were currently used to paying a lot more every month toward debt, and their property taxes were double those on their new home. With fewer expenses, they could upgrade their new home, continue to travel, or even start another savings program. Debbie was also very excited about the idea of broadening her art career and perhaps growing her business as she had once dreamed of.

This is not what happened. Greg and Debbie did list their home, and it sold for $1,174,000. They agreed to a long closing so that they could find the right "forever home." Once they purchased their new home, we met to finalize their plan.

I almost fell off my chair when I saw what they had purchased. It turned out that a home was listed for sale only three streets from their current residence that Greg had always wanted to own. It was a much bigger home on a highly sought-after street. There was a lot of interest in this home, and Greg and Debbie had only planned to walk through it during the open house just to see what it looked like. Of course, they loved it, but so did many other potential buyers. Greg and Debbie got caught up in the romance of this beautiful home and found themselves competing with two other buyers when they presented their offer. Consequently, a bidding war ensued, and they were thrilled when they found out their offer had been accepted firm for $2,065,000.

Greg believed they could live in this home for the next eight years and make a larger profit than any savings portfolio once they eventually sold it. Here is how we set up their new mortgage.

$1,174,000	Sale of current residence
(62,700)	Less real estate fees and estimated legal costs
(350,000)	Pay off current high-interest mortgage
(89,000)	Pay off line of credit
(17,000)	Pay off credit cards
(21,000)	Pay off Debbie's car loan
(39,300)	Estimated land transfer tax on purchase of $2,065,000
$595,000	Proceeds from sale

$2,065,000	New home purchase (monthly taxes $1,500)
(590,000)	Funds from sale
$1,475,000	New mortgage at 3%, amortized over 25 years ($6,980 per month)

* Mortgage balance at eighth year = $1,116,000; total estimated interest paid over 8 years = $311,140.

Of course, we helped them facilitate their purchase; however, we were very worried about their future. What if rates went up? What if Greg's health changed or his employer made him retire earlier than he anticipated? What about Debbie's future art business?

All plans changed with this home purchase. If we had known that Greg was willing to pay a monthly payment of $6,980, we could have had their new estimated mortgage paid off in only three years with our original financial solution. We would have used the additional funds over the next five years to increase their savings portfolio to a very impressive $904,650. Instead, they had dramatically increased their monthly expenses and now would pay a whopping $311,140 in interest carrying costs for their new substantial mortgage. Debbie and Greg would no longer be able to afford their lavish vacations, and we were very worried that they would go into debt to carry this new home and continue their lifestyle. That is what eventually happened.

Today, Debbie and Greg have moved from their dream home, unfortunately having to sell after only two years. They were able to make a profit of approximately $93,000, but this was soon eaten up by real estate fees, home improvement debts, credit card bills, and overdue taxes. Greg was able to continue working for the full eight years with his employer, and now works on a part-time basis. Debbie has a full-time job in a clothing store in the city. Debbie and Greg now live in a condo not far from the mall where Debbie works, and they still have a small mortgage of about $185,000. They have $48,000 in savings and a net worth of $522,000.

COACH'S MESSAGE

What can I say? This is a sad story. Life cannot be wrapped up in a neat little package with a cute little bow on top. Choices and circumstances cause us to endure financial stresses and setbacks that are sometime unforeseen. It is imperative, however, that you plan early and often. Try not to get lured in by larger homes, better lifestyles, and more things that advertisers and the media try to convince us every day that we need. Life should be a fabulous journey filled with more than just monetary trophies. Life is about relationships, friendships, and treasured accomplished goals we have striven for and rejoiced at upon their completion.

I have said throughout this book: do not overextend yourself. Please do not go too deep or too fast into debt with little time to recover. My dad always told me that if you can't decide, no matter what it is, say NO. He said you will never regret it, and it might stop you from taking a risk in life that could affect you for many years. Be smart. If you are unsure, can't decide, or think that the risk might be too great, say NO.

I know you will make the right decisions for yourself and your family. Make lists, write down your goals, envision your dreams and all your aspirations. Keep moving forward, but remember, it is truly not a race. There is no finish line to be running toward at the end of your life. Most of all, plan to be happy.

Enjoy yourself and the people you love, in your well-thought-out lifestyle, and make the small steps toward your eventual debt-free retirement. You will get there!

FINAL MESSAGE FROM YOUR COACH

WHEN I ADVISE CLIENTS, THEY TYPICALLY ALREADY KNOW WHAT TO DO. They just don't want to admit it. It's simple. We need to spend less and save more. That's it. The age of smoothing it over by refinancing your mortgage to consolidate debt has to stop. Some clients I've had for many years have refinanced their mortgages multiple times to consolidate debt. Yes, they might have moved to a different home with some of those refinances, but they have always wanted to make the payment easier on their budget by keeping the mortgage amortization at twenty-five years.

Unfortunately, we can be lulled into a sense of false security, and it is the easiest sales pitch that banks make to clients: "You should combine your debt into a new mortgage to get a lower rate. Why keep all your credit card debts at higher interest rates?" The reality is, once you consolidate into your mortgage and spread out the amortization to make the monthly payment feel more manageable, you will actually pay double for your debt because of the semi-annual calculation of interest and the longevity of the mortgage. The banks then get a client with an increased mortgage, creating more interest revenue for the bank, secured by a tangible asset: your home.

It happens to almost every working-class family. Once clients no longer feel the pinch of mounting credit card balances and everything is easily packaged into a monthly mortgage payment, they slip back into their old ways and seem to be surprised when their credit is maxed again. Purchases of must-haves for the house or the kids, or new cars, create balances on credit that we sometimes can't even remember when the bank asks. It just happens. Life is expensive, right?

What are you going to do to lower your debt and save more? Become a fighter for your future, today. Right now! Have faith in yourself, and stop worrying about the past. There is no reason you can't reach your financial goals if you really want to. Don't wallow in "should haves" and "could haves." Sometimes these setbacks are exactly what you need to stop spending, regroup, and change course for the better. Once you take control of your financial future and your day-to-day expenses, you will be building a road to comfort and security. Don't you want to break free from the shackles of debt and mounting interest?

Now, I am not saying it is easy, but as you have read from the client stories in this book, you can do it if you really want to. Anything worth having is always a little difficult. If it were really easy, everyone would be retiring with tons of money. Instead, the reality is that 67% of people today entering retirement will do so with considerable debt. You have to make sacrifices and be committed to taking charge of your financial future. You can't sit on the sidelines and watch your life go by and never make provisions for your future. You also can't pick at your debt with a toothpick. If your debt is high, remember: it is you who got it there, and now you may need to pick up a shovel and start digging out of it.

Don't be afraid to rebalance your family budget once or twice—even do it three times to find the extra funds to eliminate your debt. The feelings of accomplishment and control are like nothing you can buy. It is true power!

Think of how much interest you are saving by paying off your credit sooner. In most cases, it equates to enough to buy a new car or an extravagant vacation. Remember, interest is the complacent man's silent killer. It will eat away at your potential for retirement savings without your noticing. It is like a feeding machine that eats daily, adding more interest to your balance while you sleep. Why are you perpetuating the problem? Take control, let it go, and sleep better at night.

Once you have established your CORE, the next step is to get your money making MORE money through investing. Start putting your future on the payroll and pay yourself instead of credit card companies and banks. Whether you choose to increase your wealth by increasing your income, modestly investing in the stock market, buying real estate, leverage lending, or just starting a savings account, create and choose your own path. Fear of your financial stability has no place in your future. Take the incremental steps to your goal with commitment, and the fear will dissipate with your increased self-confidence and knowledge. Most people want a world without risk, but the true risk is doing nothing. If you believe in the theory of cause and effect, that things happen for a reason, then you will believe that everything in your past has led you here. Now make a difference with your future. Choose the path that is right for you.

As you get closer to retirement, it is imperative that you avoid risky ventures and ensure that your investments are secure and well protected. You need to build a brick wall around your finances to protect your assets and prepare for the future. Review your insurance, consider a more secure fixed income investment portfolio, understand your company pension plan, find ways to eliminate your debt faster, and review all tax incentive opportunities. Unfortunately, there are many challenges that may put limits on your future, such as inflation, market volatility, employment changes, housing costs, or even personal changes that may be unavoidable. By having a plan and protecting your capital, you can insulate yourself against any hardships and create more certainty for a comfortable future.

Always remember, if you are not planning and thinking about the future, how can you expect to have one? The fact is, you should always be moving ahead, gaining ground, and aspiring for more. You will feel great about your accomplishments and milestones, big or small. Don't let worry about money have a toxic effect on the rest of your life. Believe you are worth more. Pull away from the pack and join the wealthy savers. Know where you want to go and set yourself up to get there. The confidence and security of knowing you will be okay at retirement or in the event of an unforeseen tragedy is invaluable. It will give you the power to deal with other life issues. You will be happier, more confident, and more prepared to be successful in all aspects of your life and career.

Congratulations! You are now on your way to a new, improved, financially responsible lifestyle. Dream big. Try new things. Save more. Believe in yourself. Most of all, believe you are worth it!

See you on the beach in retirement bliss!

Christine

PS Don't forget the sunscreen.

THANK YOU

A SPECIAL THANK YOU GOES OUT TO ALL MY CLIENTS WHO GAVE THEIR permission and helped write their individual stories. This book contains personal accounts and experiences of how clients attempted to increase their wealth. It was written to offer advice, and the views in it are those of the author and the individual participants of each story. Any reference to anyone else, alive or dead, is purely coincidental.

This book is intended as a tool that, as shown in the stories and examples provided, has proved to be very successful. Neither the author, our clients, nor anyone involved in the publishing of this book accepts any liability for losses or damages incurred as a result of following the advice and details provided herein. Timing, personal circumstances, and plain old blind luck can, and often do, play a role in the outcome.

Any references in this book to retail banking products, lenders, credit rules, banks, and investment and insurance products are offered only as examples, and are in no way meant to endorse or specifically recommend any specific lender, method, product, or tool.

We realize that everyone's personal situation is unique, and we recommend seeking advice from your advisors when planning your future. Please consider attending one of our Focus-Groups on Building Wealth—we would love to meet you. You can also email us at: debtfreewealthy@gmail.com.

Good luck and best wishes,

Chris